For Janine

Enjoy and have fun
in the kitchen!

Anabel Legben

may 2004.

Feeling relaxed and comfortable

in someone else's home and enjoying food they have

prepared (no matter how simple) is one of life's

great pleasures. Sharing our table returns us to

a tradition that has nourished mankind for centuries.

In the complex times we live in, there's still no better

way to revive and grow the bonds

of friendship and kinship.

DEDICATION ...

For my lovely mother Anne, an inspiring cook.

AN ANNABEL LANGBEIN BOOK

First published in 2003 by Annabel Langbein Books.
An imprint of The International Culinary Institute Press Ltd,
PO Box 99068 Newmarket, Auckland, New Zealand

ISBN 0-9582029-5-8

FOOD STYLING Annabel Langbein
TABLESETTINGS AND PROPS Sarah Lods
DESIGN & PRODUCTION MANAGEMENT Karryn Muschamp
COPY EDITOR Sally Butters
TYPESETTING Natalie Keys for ICIP
Printed in China through Colorcraft Ltd., Hong Kong

Visit Annabel's website:
www.annabel-langbein.com

cooking
to impress WITHOUT STRESS

annabel langbein
photography nick tresidder

annabel langbein books

CONTENTS

THE 12 COMMANDMENTS

1 CONFIDENCE IS EVERYTHING.
Even if you don't spend much time
in the kitchen or you live life on the run,
it's not difficult to put a stunning meal
on the table. Believe you can do it.

2 COOK IN YOUR COMFORT ZONE.
Choose foods that you like to cook
and eat, and don't get tricky with a new,
untried idea. Your home is not
a restaurant and you are not a chef.

3 KNOW YOUR AUDIENCE.
Find out before they arrive if there is
anything they won't or can't eat.

**4 DESIGN A MENU AROUND THE
SEASONS**, your budget and any flavour
preferences. Buy the best quality
ingredients, preferably organic, from
suppliers you trust.

5 IF YOU ARE SHORT ON TIME
or not up to cooking a lot, buy really
good quality ready-made foods and
create meals that you can more or
less "assemble".

**6 LIE THROUGH YOUR TEETH ABOUT
#5.** A friend (an excellent cook who is
frequently called on to entertain people
at the drop of a hat) often buys in a
good meat pie and burns it slightly
before serving it. People rave about her
fabulous pies.

7 AVOID LAST-MINUTE PANIC.
Plan ahead, make lists, do whatever you
can ahead of time.

**8 CREATE THE ILLUSION OF
CONTROL.** Appearances are everything.
Set the table beautifully before guests
arrive and slip into something gorgeous.

9 DELEGATE.
Remind your partner, should you have
one, that they are not a guest here and
you need their help.

10 DON'T FALL INTO THE GRAVY.
Remember that too many chardonnays
ruin the cook.

11 TASTE EVERYTHING – as you cook
and before you serve.

**12 ACCEPT COMPLIMENTS
GRACIOUSLY,** offer no apologies and
don't forget to enjoy yourself.

GETTING ORGANISED

WINE AND OTHER DRINKS

Certain wine and food matches make the palate soar. Creating food and wine matches that work is not so much a matter of choosing whether to serve a white wine or a red, but more about the balance between the dish and the wine. If the wine is big and gutsy and the food is delicate, the dish will be overpowered and taste insignificant, and vice versa.

Usually when we dine we start with something light to stimulate the palate then move on to food that is richer, heavier and more intensely flavoured, and so the progression should be with the wines served.

Tannin works to cut fat on the palate (in the same way cream softens the tannins and bitterness of coffee) so if you are serving a rich meat dish you are best off with a big tannic wine – something like a weighty Australian shiraz. Find a delicate, ravishingly perfumed riesling or pinot gris to serve with a flash-roasted scallop or gently poached chicken dish.

GUEST NUMBERS

The recipes in this book have mostly been written for 4-6 people. However, they can be scaled up or down as needed, whether you are having a birthday party, weekend lunch or smart Saturday night sit-down dinner, or you want to create an intimate dinner for two. You'll find menu suggestions at the back of the book in the menu planning section (pages 144-153).

USING THE RECIPES

If you are new to cooking follow the recipe closely like a road map. That way you will end up at the right place and with a dish you feel pleased about. As you gain confidence take your own cues and use the recipes more as a guide. Choose one system for measuring – whether it is by weight or by cup – and stick to it, don't mix and match. Use a timer for rice, pasta, bread and any other baking. It's easy to get distracted and suddenly find something is ruined just because you forgot to put the timer on. However you choose to cook, taste your food as you go and adjust the seasonings to suit – this is your food when you serve it up, not the recipe book's.

INGREDIENTS

Don't be put off from trying a recipe if you don't have all the ingredients on hand. Substitute ingredients or omit them – if a sauce calls for fennel and you don't have any or don't like fennel, leave it out. The flavour won't be quite the same but unless the dish is based around fennel it won't really matter. Part of cooking is being able to improvise or adapt a recipe to suit – you never know what you will discover.

SERVING

Most of the time I like to plate food in the kitchen. That way I can portion the main protein (and make sure there is enough), check the plates are hot and get each plate looking the way I want it. Side dishes of vegetables, salad and the like go on the table for people to pass around. This allows for some personal interchange and lets guests have some say about what they put on their plates. If there's a big pie or an impressive roast it's nice to serve it at the table or let people help themselves. Just try to avoid a lot of clutter on the table or having to pass around big, heavy and hot dishes.

CREATING A MENU

Throughout the book you will find a numbered menu symbol.

This indicates that the recipe is part of a menu, the instructions for which can be found on pages 144-153.

SETTING THE SCENE

Light candles, arrange some fresh flowers and set a gorgeous table. Even if you haven't cooked a thing, provided the table is carefully set and you look organised and relaxed, people will feel welcome when they arrive.

It does not take much effort or money to give the impression that you have gone to a lot of trouble. Appearances are everything. On a beautifully laid table even the simplest food feels special. Stunning food does not equate to complicated, rich or extravagant ingredients.

Light a fragrant candle in the bathroom and leave the door open. If you have a big house shut other doors so your guests don't get lost en route to the bathroom and perhaps, heaven forbid, discover that you failed Housekeeping 101.

If it's getting wintry, light a fire or put on some heat – people can't feel comfortable or relaxed if they are cold.

Take a break from the kitchen an hour or two before guests arrive, otherwise you will be sick to death of the sight of food before you have even started. Before guests arrive throw some bread, bacon or something garlicky into the oven to create a tummy-warming aroma and make the house smell comfortable and inviting. The following spiced almonds do just the trick.

SPICED ALMONDS: Toss 2 cups raw almonds with 1 tsp oil, 1 tsp garlic salt, 1 tsp commercial Moroccan spice, 1/2 tsp salt and a pinch of chilli powder in a large roasting dish. Bake at 180°C / 350°F for 20 minutes or until nuts are crisp and aromatic. Cool and serve or store in an airtight container. Makes 2 cups.

ON ARRIVAL

SMOKY BABA GHANOUSH

1 large or 2 medium eggplants
6 cloves garlic, unpeeled
1/2 cup olive oil
3 tbsp lemon juice
3/4 tsp salt, sprinkle of pepper
1 tbsp chopped parsley or basil

Heat oven to 250°C / 500°F. Place eggplant in a shallow baking tray and bake 35-40 minutes or until skin has blackened and eggplant has collapsed. Add garlic to dish, reduce heat to 200°C / 400°F and bake 15 minutes. Cool. Remove skins from garlic and eggplant. Squeeze the eggplant over the sink to remove liquid from flesh. Purée garlic and eggplant flesh with all other ingredients until smooth and creamy. Store in a covered container in the fridge. It will keep for about a week.

The best way to break the ice when guests arrive is to bring them into the kitchen or outside onto the deck where they can stand and mill around, rather than sitting them down in a formal living room. It feels far more relaxed. You might like to serve a cocktail or some cold bubbly or chilled still wine. Always make sure non-alcoholic drinks are available and have a big jug of iced water and glasses at hand for people to help themselves.

Whet guests' appetites with little snacks. Tip wasabi peas, pistachios and roasted nuts out of the packets and into bowls. Buy or make dips and make up a platter with crispbreads and olives. There's a terrific recipe for Pita Bread Crisps on page 20.

MARINATED OLIVES: I like to flavour olives with a sprig of rosemary, a clove or two of garlic and a fresh chilli. Mix through 2-3 cups olives, add 1/2 cup olive oil and heat in the microwave for 3-4 minutes to infuse flavours. Store olives in oil in the fridge. They will keep for several weeks.

RIGHT: Pita Bread Crisps with
Smoky Baba Ghanoush and Marinated Olives.

STARTERS & SMALL PLATES

Elevating an everyday meal to a special occasion doesn't demand a departure to complicated dishes or ones different to those we know and love and enjoy. It's the ambience you create that allows people to feel relaxed and spoilt. You can go to all the trouble in the world in the kitchen but if your dining room is chilly, a fluorescent light is blaring and the food is slopped onto cold plates without napkins, water glasses or any sense of table setting – well, you may as well not have bothered. Presentation and delivery are key.

One of the easiest ways to make a meal feel special is to include a first course. A lovely light zucchini soup, roasted beet or grilled fig salad, or a plate of little chilli and coconut spiked chicken fritters will provide a culinary hike to any meal and also stimulate our social appetite – a small, pleasing taste awaiting at the table signals the time for everyone to relax and enjoy a good time.

For lunch or a late supper I often like to serve a couple of small plates rather than one hefty, meaty main course – soup with a salad, a big bowl of steaming mussels and some yummy homemade bread, or perhaps a plate of slow-roasted tomatoes and marinated mozzarella followed by a spicy chicken cake or a tender little onion tart. Little plates offering generous tastes is my favourite way to eat. There's a sense of titillating the appetite without jading the palate. Mix and match the following selection or, if time is not on your side, take some cues from the simple assembly ideas scattered throughout this chapter.

LEFT: Balsamic Caramelised Onion Tart (recipe page 18)

SAVOURY FLAKY PASTRY

Makes 550g / 20oz. Allow about 45g / 1.5oz pastry per single-serve tart.

2 cups flour
2 tsp sugar
1/2 tsp salt
150g / 5oz butter, cut in small pieces
1/4 cup cold water

Place flour, sugar, salt and butter in the bowl of a food processor and blitz to a fine crumb. With motor running, add water only until mixture comes together in a ball. Remove from bowl and work lightly with hands until smooth. Press out to a rough rectangle, wrap in plastic and chill or freeze before rolling out and baking.

SAVOURY TARTS

A tender tart makes great lunch fare or a starter before a light meal. You can use commercial pastry but it's incredibly easy to make your own – especially with a food processor – and the recipe in the panel makes a good amount that will keep chilled for several days or can be frozen. A simple salad of rocket (arugula) leaves and avocado wedges dressed with Balsamic Dressing (page 22) makes a good partner to any savoury tart.

BALSAMIC CARAMELISED ONION TARTS

MAKES: 6 tarts PREP TIME: 10 minutes COOK TIME: 20-22 minutes
MAKE AHEAD: pastry and onions can both be prepared several days in advance and pastry can be frozen

250g / 8oz Savoury Flaky Pastry (see side panel),
or 1 1/2 sheets commercial savoury pastry
6 tsp olive paste or tapenade
1 cup Balsamic Caramel Onions (page 97)
80g / 3oz / 1/3 cup goats' cheese or feta, crumbled
3-4 anchovies, cut into small strips
GARNISH: 6 tiny sprigs fresh rosemary

HEAT oven to 200°C / 400°F. Roll pastry thinly between 2 sheets of heavy duty plastic wrap or teflon paper to 3mm / 1/8 inch thickness and cut into six 11-12cm / 4 inch rounds. Place on a baking tray lined with baking parchment. Spread each round with a teaspoon of olive paste. Spread a heaped tablespoon of caramelised onions on top.

SPRINKLE with cheese and a little anchovy and garnish with rosemary sprigs. Bake 10 minutes then reduce heat to 170°C / 325°F and bake another 10-12 minutes or until tarts are golden and pastry is cooked through.

PASTRY CUT-OUTS:
These are useful as a garnish for stews or as an alternative to a whole pastry crust. Roll out Savoury Flaky Pastry (see side panel) to 1/2cm / 1/4 inch thickness or use commercial pastry. Cut into triangles or shapes of your choice. If desired, garnish the top of each cut-out with leaf or flower pastry shapes. Brush with beaten egg and bake 20 minutes at 180°C / 350°F.

ROASTED TOMATO AND BASIL TARTS

◇ 250g / 8oz Savoury Flaky Pastry (see opposite page), rolled thinly ◇ 3 Italian tomatoes, sliced ◇ salt and freshly ground black pepper ◇ 150g / 5oz fresh mozzarella, sliced ◇ 6 tsp basil oil (page 30) or pesto thinned with olive oil

Heat oven to 220°C / 425°F. Place six 12cm / 4 inch rounds of pastry on a baking tray. Overlap slices of tomato and cheese on top of each one. Season well and drizzle each with 1 teaspoon basil oil. Bake 6-7 minutes then reduce heat to 180°C / 350°F and bake a further 15-20 minutes.

ASPARAGUS TARTS

You can use asparagus, zucchini or red capsicums (bell peppers) for these tarts.

◇ 1 sheet puff pastry ◇ 4 tsp olive paste (optional) ◇ 100g / ½ cup goats' cheese or feta ◇ 16 trimmed asparagus spears ◇ finely grated zest of ½ lemon ◇ salt and ground black pepper ◇ olive oil spray

Heat oven to 200°C / 400°F. Cut pastry into 8 even rectangles and place on a baking tray lined with baking parchment. Spread with olive paste. Crumble or slice cheese over top. Place 2 asparagus spears on top of each rectangle. Grate over a little lemon zest, season and spray with a little oil spray. Bake 15-20 minutes or until golden and pastry is cooked through. Serve warm.

TUSCAN ZUCCHINI SOUP

SERVES: 6 PREP TIME: 10 minutes COOK TIME: 20 minutes
MAKE AHEAD: up to 2 days

I first enjoyed this light, satisfying soup at a lunch cooked by Australian chef Neil Perry. I have adapted his recipe slightly and omitted any cream as I find the soup pleasingly rounded and unctuous without it. Choose best quality parmesan cheese and grate it from the block. I always like to make extra soup to have in the fridge for an easy home-alone lunch or a light supper. This soup keeps in the fridge for a couple of days but don't freeze it as it will lose its pretty, fresh green colour.

> 1kg / about 2 lb small green zucchini
> 3 tbsp extra virgin olive oil
> 4 cloves garlic, finely chopped
> 30-40 basil leaves, chopped
> 1 tsp salt and several grinds black pepper
> 4 cups chicken or vegetable stock
> 1 tbsp chopped Italian parsley
> 50g parmesan, finely grated

CUT zucchini lengthways into quarters then into 1cm / ½ inch dice. Heat oil in a heavy-based saucepan. Add zucchini, garlic, basil, salt and pepper. Cook over low heat for 10 minutes or until zucchini have softened.

REMOVE ⅓ cup zucchini and reserve for garnishing soup. Add stock to remaining zucchini and simmer over medium heat 8 minutes or until zucchini are very soft and transparent. Purée in batches in a food processor until smooth then return to saucepan. Adjust seasoning to taste. Cool, cover and chill if not serving at once.

TO SERVE: Stir in parsley and parmesan and bring to just below a simmer. Ladle soup into 6 warm bowls and top with a spoonful of reserved zucchini. Serve immediately. Accompany with Pita Bread Crisps (see side panel).

PITA BREAD CRISPS

You can buy excellent commercial versions of these crisps but if I have the time I like to make my own. As they say, you get more bite for your buck.

Heat oven to 160°C / 325°F. Blend to a fine purée: ⅔ cup olive oil, 3 tbsp grated parmesan, 1 tsp dried oregano, 3 cloves garlic, roughly chopped and ½ tsp salt. Split 6-8 large, round pita breads and liberally brush inside surfaces with oil mixture. Cut into wedges and arrange in a single layer on baking trays. Bake about 30 minutes or until golden and crisp. Store in an airtight container when cool.

menu 5

Don't seat all the bright, chatty people up one end of the table and the quiet ones at the other. (You can, however, sit at the opposite end of someone your partner has invited who you find utterly tedious.) Mix people up and don't seat people who arrived together next to each other. If there are more than 8 people it's a good idea to use place names for seating so you can put people where you want them without having to remember it all in your head.

DRINKS ON THE TABLE
Keep glasses replenished with fresh, chilled water throughout the meal. There's an old rule that says make the first bottle of wine the best. In other words, don't raid the cellar late and tiddly – no one will have any idea how incredibly divine that 1970 Chateau Latour really was.

MUSIC
Set up the music you want before guests arrive, deciding on the feel you want for the night. Is this a Barry White/Marvin Gaye night or a Vivaldi evening. Keep the noise level low enough so you can hold an easy conversation, unless you want everyone to abandon the food and start dancing.

menu

PROSCIUTTO FIG SALAD

SERVES: 6 PREP TIME: 10 minutes COOK TIME: 5 minutes
MAKE AHEAD: balsamic dressing can be made up to 5 days ahead and chilled; figs can be grilled up to 8 hours ahead

When figs are in season, it's hard to get enough of them if you are a fig lover. Sometimes I wrap the figs in prosciutto and eat them as little roll-ups, other times I dip them into balsamic vinegar and throw them under the grill. Here, grilled with maple syrup and served in a tasty little salad with a swirl of prosciutto, they make an elegant light lunch or first course for dinner. If fig season has been and gone make this salad with sliced pears that have been drizzled with a little maple syrup before grilling.

9 fresh figs, halved
1 tsp balsamic vinegar
1 tsp maple syrup
150g / 5oz mixed salad greens, washed and dried
80-100g / 3-4oz blue cheese, crumbled
6 slices prosciutto or crispy fried bacon

BALSAMIC DRESSING
3 tbsp olive oil
1 tbsp balsamic vinegar
1 tsp Dijon mustard
1/2 tsp sugar
salt and pepper

BRUSH figs with combined vinegar and maple syrup. Place under a heated grill for about 5 minutes or until lightly golden and starting to soften. Cool.

COMBINE dressing ingredients and toss through salad greens. Divide between 6 serving plates. Top each plate with 3 fig halves and a sprinkling of blue cheese. Fold prosciutto and place on top or sprinkle with crumbled bacon.

◇ FIGS WITH GORGONZOLA SAUCE: Halve fresh figs and drizzle with warm Creamy Gorgonzola Sauce (page 107). Top with crispy fried, crumbled prosciutto.

NO COOK STARTERS

When you want to serve a starter but don't have a lot of time, try one of these fresh, light assembly ideas for a first course that doesn't require any cooking.

 menu ②

SPIKED PRAWN COCKTAIL

You could also go for the retro version – make a dressing of tomato ketchup mixed through whipped cream with a little lemon juice – but I like the clean zing of Vietnamese Dressing.

Combine 200g / 7oz cooked prawns or shrimps with 2-3 finely shredded iceberg lettuce leaves, 1 grated carrot and 12 shredded mint leaves. Divide between 4 cocktail glasses. Spoon 1 tbsp Vietnamese Dressing (page 82) over each one. Top with a prawn tail and garnish with Spring Onion Curls.

SPRING ONION CURLS: Cut the green section of spring onions into 5-8cm / 2-3 inch lengths. Cut into very thin strips. Place in a bowl of iced water to curl.

SHRIMP SHOOTERS

My mother was a terrific entertainer in her time. When I was growing up dinners for twenty or more guests seemed a frequent occurrence. Shrimp shooters sometimes featured as a pre-dinner snack. I've brought the idea out of the Sixties with wasabi and vodka. Leave out the vodka if preferred.

Combine 1 cup chilled tomato juice with 2-3 tbsp chilled vodka, 1 tsp wasabi paste, 2 tbsp lemon juice and 1 tsp soy sauce. Mix in 184g / 6oz can small shrimps, drained, or 150g / 5oz chopped cooked prawn meat. Season to taste with salt and pepper. Serve in shooter glasses. Serves 6-8.

◇ OYSTER SHOOTERS: Replace shrimps with fresh oysters.

CEVICHE – SOUTH AMERICAN MARINATED FISH

The fish for this refreshing salad needs to marinate for at least 6 hours. Add other ingredients at serving time.

For 6 people allow 500g / ½ lb freshest, boneless, skinless fish. Slice fish very thinly across the grain and place in a non-corrosive bowl with enough fresh lime juice to just cover (about ½ cup). Chill for at least 6 hours or up to 12 hours. At serving time, drain off juices and add the chopped flesh of 1 just-ripe avocado, 1 finely diced red chilli, the finely chopped greens of 1 spring onion, 2 tbsp chopped coriander (cilantro) and 2 tsp olive oil. Season with salt and pepper and serve.

◇ VARIATION: Pacific Ceviche – add ½ cup coconut cream to salad in place of olive oil.

CAESAR SALAD

A classic, but a goodie. Make the dressing in advance, ready for a speedy assembly.

For 6 people allow about 40 baby cos lettuce leaves, 24 Crostini (page 32), 6 slices crispy fried bacon or prosciutto, about 30 shavings of fresh parmesan cut with a vegetable peeler and 1 recipe Caesar Salad Dressing. Place lettuce, crostini and bacon on serving plates. Shave over parmesan and drizzle with dressing.

CAESAR SALAD DRESSING

Shake together 2 tbsp olive oil, 5-6 finely chopped anchovies, 2 cloves crushed garlic, ½ cup cream and 2 tbsp lemon juice. This will keep in the fridge 2-3 days.

PLATTER OF FENNEL SALAD, TUNA TARTARE AND ROASTED STUFFED CAPSICUMS

SERVES: 6 PREP TIME: 10 minutes plus salting for fennel, 5 minutes for tuna
MAKE AHEAD: up to 4 hours for tuna if kept well chilled, and 24 hours for fennel

The components for this elegant platter can be made ahead, ready to assemble at serving time. The three items shown here are a particularly pleasing combination but you could easily serve any one of them as a stand-alone starter.

	2-3 small firm heads fennel, washed
FENNEL	2 tsp salt
SALAD	1 tbsp chopped fresh mint (about 16-20 leaves)
	50g / 2oz parmesan or pecorino cheese, shaved with a potato peeler
	2 tbsp extra virgin olive oil
	juice of 1/2 lemon
	freshly ground black pepper

CUT fennel heads in half lengthways and trim off tough bases. Slice fennel as finely as possible, starting from cut surfaces (use a Benriner slicer or potato peeler). Place in a non-corrosive bowl, sprinkle with salt and mix through. Stand 15-20 minutes.

RINSE fennel very well until it no longer tastes over-salty. Drain thoroughly and mix in mint, parmesan and oil. Chill until ready to serve. At serving time mix through lemon juice and grind over black pepper.

TUNA	300g / 11oz freshest tuna loin or belly, any tough white connective
TARTARE	tissue cut off and discarded
	finely grated zest of 1 lemon or lime
	1 tbsp extra virgin olive oil
	TO SERVE: juice of 1/2 lime or lemon, salt and freshly ground
	black pepper

CUT tuna into very fine slivers – use a very sharp knife so it cuts rather than mashes the flesh. Mix through zest and oil and chill in a covered container until ready to serve. At serving time, mix through lime or lemon juice and season with salt and pepper.

◇ ASIAN-STYLED TUNA TARTARE: Add 1 tbsp chopped fresh mint leaves and 1/4 tsp minced fresh chilli with lemon or lime zest and oil.

ROASTED STUFFED CAPSICUMS: Recipe page 96.

RIGHT: Fennel Salad, Tuna Tartare and Roasted Stuffed Capsicums.

menu ①

SPEEDY OYSTER ASSEMBLIES

Most oyster lovers agree that fresh oysters need nothing more than a grind of black pepper and a squeeze of lemon, or a quick dunk into balsamic vinegar to complement their sweet, briny flavour. If you feel like something smarter, try any of the following dressings. Each recipe makes enough for 2 dozen oysters. The tasty bread swirls are good to sit oysters on.

SHINTO DRESSING
Combine ¼ cup rice vinegar, 2 tbsp dry sherry, 1 tsp fish sauce, 1 tbsp finely chopped coriander (cilantro), ½ tsp finely chopped chilli and ½ tsp each of sugar, grated fresh ginger and sesame oil. Just before serving spoon a teaspoon of sauce over each oyster.

PROVENÇALE DRESSING
Whisk together until smooth and emulsified: 1 fresh egg yolk, 1 clove crushed garlic, 2 tsp Dijon mustard, 50ml / ¼ cup white wine vinegar and 150ml / 5oz grapeseed oil. Season with salt and pepper. Just before serving spoon a teaspoon of sauce over each oyster. Garnish with shredded cucumber. Makes ¾ cup dressing.

PICO DE GALLO
Combine 2 large tomatoes, cut in 1cm / ½ inch cubes, with 1 small, finely diced onion, 4 minced cloves garlic, 2 minced chillies, 4 tbsp chopped coriander (cilantro), 2 tbsp lime juice, 2 tbsp olive oil, and salt and a pinch of sugar to taste. Stand 30 minutes. Just before serving spoon a teaspoon of sauce over each oyster.

LEMON WASABI SWIRLS
Tradition sees fresh oysters served with thinly sliced bread and butter. Take a tangent with a little wasabi in the butter or make these simple swirls.

Combine 100g / 3½oz butter with the finely grated zest of ½ lemon, 2 tbsp chopped soft herbs (eg chives, parsley or coriander/cilantro) and 2 tsp wasabi paste. Spread over 16 thin slices of white or soft wholemeal bread. Firmly roll up bread into cylinders and secure with toothpicks. Chill until firm then cut off crust ends and slice each roll into 3cm / 1 inch pieces. Top each roll with a fresh oyster.

LEFT: Fresh Oysters served with balsamic vinegar.

SPICY CHICKEN CAKES

MAKES: about 20 medium or 30 small cakes PREP TIME: 10 minutes
COOK TIME: 4-6 minutes (per batch)
MAKE AHEAD: can be made up to a day ahead and kept chilled; reheat quickly in a
hot oven

A food processor makes fast work of these tasty little chicken cakes. The coconut cream in the mixture makes them brown quickly so take care when cooking not to burn the outside before the centres are fully cooked (it is important to cook them right through). If I am making a big batch for a party I like to brown the cakes quickly in the pan then finish cooking them in the oven – pop them on a baking tray and into a hot oven for 5-6 minutes or until they are springy to the touch.

> 300g / 11oz lean skinless chicken, roughly chopped
> small handful coriander (cilantro) leaves
> 1 spring (green) onion, finely sliced
> finely grated zest of 1 lime or lemon (no pith)
> 2 tbsp sweet Thai chilli sauce
> 2 tsp fish sauce
> 1 egg white
> salt and freshly ground black pepper
> 1/4 cup coconut cream
> flavourless oil (eg grapeseed) for frying
> OPTIONAL TO SERVE: Avocado Salsa,
>   Basil Oil (see side panel), rocket (arugula) leaves

PLACE all ingredients, except coconut cream and oil, in a food processor and blend to a coarse purée. With motor running, add coconut cream in a slow stream and mix until evenly combined.

HEAT a lightly oiled frypan and cook small spoonfuls of mixture 2-3 minutes each side over medium heat until cooked through and springy to the touch. Serve on rocket leaves and accompany with Avocado Salsa. Spoon around Basil Oil.

COOK'S NOTE: This recipe can also be prepared with raw prawn meat or fish.

AVOCADO SALSA

Combine 1 large, firm avocado, finely diced, 1 small chilli, seeded and finely chopped or 1 tsp chilli sauce, 2 tbsp lemon juice and salt and freshly ground black pepper.

Prepare just before serving. Makes about 1 cup.

BASIL OIL

This soft, unctuous flavouring is made in a flash. It is ideally suited to poached, grilled or panfried fish and is equally delicious on boiled potatoes and grilled or steamed vegetables.

Pour boiling water over 1 tightly packed cup basil leaves. Drain at once and refresh under cold water. Drain thoroughly and purée with 1/2 tsp salt and 1/2 cup extra virgin olive oil until smooth. Store in the fridge – it will keep 4-5 days – or freeze in ice block containers. Makes 3/4 cup.

CORIANDER OR MINT OIL

Use any soft herbs to make the oil, including coriander, mint, chervil and parsley. Follow the method for basil oil. Add nuts, garlic and parmesan for a pesto.

SALAD OF BEETS, BEANS, WALNUTS
AND GOATS' CHEESE

SERVES: 4 PREP TIME: 10 minutes COOK TIME: 40 minutes
MAKE AHEAD: all the components can be prepared ahead, ready for a quick, last-minute assembly

This is a lovely salad to make at the start of spring and serve before a big, hearty dinner stew or pie, or in duo with a savoury tart or soup for a smart lunch. I adore roasted beets – their sweet, caramelly flavour is quite addictive. As a side dish you can simplify things using just roasted beets, rocket (arugula) and walnuts.

> 4-6 (about 600g / 1¼ lb) small beetroot (beets), peeled and cut
>   into 6-8 wedges
> 1 tbsp brown sugar
> 2 tbsp balsamic vinegar
> ¼ cup extra virgin olive oil
> salt and freshly ground black pepper
> ¾ cup walnut pieces
> 4 handfuls fresh rocket (arugula) or watercress, coarse stems removed
> 1 cup peeled broad beans or frozen green soya beans, thawed
>   (about 2 cups unpeeled)
> 100g / 3½ oz goats' cheese, sheep's cheese or feta

HEAT oven to 180°C / 350°F. Place beetroot in a shallow roasting pan lined with baking parchment. Mix through sugar, vinegar and oil and season with salt and pepper. Spread out to a single layer and roast 40 minutes or until tender and starting to shrivel. Leave in pan to cool.

TOAST walnuts in a separate roasting dish for 15 minutes at the same temperature. Add walnuts, rocket leaves and beans to cooled beetroot and toss to coat in pan oils. Divide between 4 serving plates. Slice cheese over the top.

◇ COOK'S NOTE: Broad beans and soya beans both have a short season but are always available frozen. Frozen broad beans can be popped straight out of their skins. Fresh broad beans must first be podded then blanched in boiling water for 2 minutes before peeling off the greyish outer skin.
◇ Walnuts turn rancid very quickly. Always check the smell before using.

CROSTINI

Crunchy crostini make a terrific garnish for a salad or can be served with a little savoury topping as an appetiser.

Cut 2cm / 1 inch slices of **French or rustic country bread** on an angle. Place on a baking tray and brush liberally with **extra virgin olive oil**. Bake at 180°C / 350°F for about 15 minutes until crisp. Cool and store in an airtight container. These will keep for several weeks. Re-crisp in oven for 5 minutes to freshen if required.

MUSSELS

Mussels make an easy, appealing starter, steamed open in an aromatic broth or sauce. Scrub and remove beards from mussels before cooking. Discard any with broken shells or that stay open when tapped or run under cold water. After cooking, throw away any that don't open. The following recipes all serve 6 people for a starter or 4 for a main course.

SAKE AND GINGER MUSSELS
The zing of this fresh sauce is a terrific accompaniment to the sweet mussel flesh – and there's no added fat.

Clean 3 dozen mussels. In a large, heavy pot place ¼ cup sake, ¼ cup sweet Thai chilli sauce, ½ cup water, 2 tsp grated fresh ginger and 2 spring (green) onions, finely chopped. Add mussels, cover and cook until they open, removing them as they do. Pile into a bowl. Add 2 tbsp lemon juice, 2 tbsp chopped coriander (cilantro) and an extra teaspoon of grated, fresh ginger to pan juices and pour over mussels.

MUSSELS IN GARLIC CREAM SAUCE
The traditional moules à la marinière with garlic, herbs and white wine gets a voluptuous touch with a dollop of cream.

Clean 3 dozen mussels. Heat 1 tbsp butter in a pan and sizzle 2 large cloves minced garlic for a few seconds. Add ½ cup fruity white wine such as riesling and bring to a fast boil. Add mussels and cover and cook until they open, removing them as they do. Add ½ cup cream to pan juices and boil hard until lightly thickened. Add cooked mussels back to sauce and heat for a minute to warm through. Pile cooked mussels into a serving dish. Season sauce with pepper, add a small handful chopped parsley (no salt should be needed as mussel juices tend to be salty) and spoon over mussels. Accompany with crusty bread. Variation: Creamy Mussel Soup – purée mussel meat and sauce to produce a wonderful mussel soup.

MUSSELS IN NAPOLETANO BROTH
Part and parcel of those hole-in-the-wall, checked tablecloth and Chianti bottle establishments, but nevertheless a dish that never goes out of fashion.

Clean 3 dozen mussels. Heat 1 tbsp olive oil and sizzle 2 minced cloves garlic for a few seconds. Add a 400g / 15oz can chopped tomatoes in juice, 1 tsp honey, 2 tbsp vermouth, 3 tbsp chopped fresh herbs such as parsley, oregano, thyme and ½ cup cream. Bring to a boil, add mussels, cover and cook, removing mussels as they open. Pile cooked mussels into a serving dish. Pour over sauce.

LEFT: Sake and Ginger Mussels

Prepare as for slow roasted vine tomatoes opposite, using 1 kg / 2 lb large tomatoes, cored and quartered. Double the flavourings and increase the cooking time to about 2 hours or until tomatoes are shrivelled. Store in the fridge. They will keep for about a week.

USING SLOW ROASTED TOMATOES

• Fragrant Tomato Soup - make a double recipe of slow roasted tomatoes, remove skins and purée. Heat with chicken stock and serve drizzled with Basil Oil (page 30) and garnished with parmesan.

• Roast Tomato Pasta - toss slow roasted tomatoes through cooked pasta with spinach and goats' cheese.

• Roast Tomato Tart - serve slow roasted tomatoes in a cooked savoury tart case (page 18) with crumbled blue cheese and finely shredded sorrel or rocket (arugula) leaves.

SLOW ROASTED VINE TOMATOES WITH FRESH MOZZARELLA SALAD

SERVES: 6 PREP TIME: 5 minutes COOK TIME: 1 hour
MAKE AHEAD: tomatoes can be roasted the morning of serving; marinate cheese several hours ahead

The tomatoes in this delicious dish offer a melt-in-the-mouth juiciness. I usually serve them with a small soup spoon and some bread to mop up the juices. It's a light but delicious combination that is really good to make in autumn when tomatoes are at their sweetest. Allow 3 tomatoes per serving, but if you like prepare a double recipe as they keep in the fridge for several days and can be whizzed up and heated for an instant pasta, steak sauce or soup (see side panel). Partnered with a fresh mozzarella salad they make a terrific first course to precede a roast or stew, or a light autumn lunch, followed by Tuscan Zucchini Soup (page 20).

18 small vine tomatoes, on the vine
¼ cup extra virgin olive oil
2 tbsp balsamic vinegar
pinch each salt and pepper
2 tsp sugar

MOZZARELLA SALAD
150g-200g / 5-7oz fresh mozzarella or bocconcini
3 tbsp extra virgin olive oil
salt and freshly ground black pepper
20-24 small basil leaves

HEAT oven to 150°C / 300°F. Carefully cut vines into bunches of 3-4 tomatoes. Place on a baking tray lined with baking parchment. Drizzle with oil and vinegar, season with salt and pepper and sprinkle with sugar. Bake 1 hour or until slightly shrivelled. Leave on tray until ready to serve.

MOZZARELLA SALAD Slice cheese thinly and combine with oil. Season with salt and pepper. Toss through basil just before serving. Serve a branch of tomatoes with a little of the balsamic juices spooned over. Spoon cheese salad to the side and drizzle over oil from salad. Serve salad at room temperature.

◇ NO COOK TOMATO AND MOZZARELLA SALAD: Use commercial semi-dried tomatoes and mix with sliced mozzarella and basil and a little extra virgin olive oil. Season with salt and pepper.

ASPARAGUS AND SCALLOP SALAD WITH CITRUS CHILLI DRESSING

SERVES: 2 PREP TIME: 5 minutes COOK TIME: 3 minutes
MAKE AHEAD: make dressing up to a week ahead; cook asparagus up to 2 hours ahead; cook scallops up to half hour ahead

CITRUS CHILLI DRESSING

Make this dressing in bulk for a zingy fat-free flavour boost for salads, seafood and noodles. It will keep in the fridge for up to a week.

1/3 cup fresh lemon or lime juice
1/4 cup fresh orange juice
1 tbsp rice vinegar
2 tbsp fish sauce
1 small red chilli, seeds removed and flesh finely sliced
1 tbsp sugar

Mix all ingredients together and chill until ready to serve. Makes 1 small cup.

Make the most of tender asparagus during its short spring season. A big platter piled with freshly cooked spears drizzled with lemon-infused olive oil makes a speedy first course, but for a special treat check out this stunning asparagus and scallop salad. It is just the trick for a romantic dinner a deux, or double the recipe for a special occasion dinner for friends. Even the freshest asparagus has tough stems – to remove simply snap the asparagus and discard the tough ends. Take care not to over-cook – it takes only 3 minutes.

> 8-10 spears fresh asparagus, tough ends snapped off and discarded
> 10-16 fresh scallops (as extravagance allows)
> finely grated zest of 1/2 lemon or lime
> salt and freshly ground black pepper
> pinch sugar
> 1 tbsp olive oil
> 1/4 cup Citrus Chilli Dressing – see side panel
> TO SERVE: handful fresh basil leaves (or mint or coriander/cilantro when basil is not available), flesh of 1 just ripe avocado cut into chunks, a little extra virgin olive oil to drizzle

DROP trimmed asparagus into a pot of lightly salted boiling water and boil 3 minutes. Refresh under cold water and drain thoroughly. Set aside.

MIX scallops with lemon zest and season with salt, pepper and sugar. Heat oil in a heavy pan until very hot and cook scallops about 1 minute each side – they should be browned but still soft. Do not overcook.

DRIZZLE warm scallops with a little dressing and toss with asparagus. Gently combine with basil and avocado. Arrange on 2 plates and spoon over remaining dressing. Drizzle a little extra virgin olive oil around the plate.

RICHARD HARRIS' SEARED SQUID AND GLASS NOODLE SALAD

MAKES: 6 serves PREP TIME: 20 minutes plus marinating COOK TIME: 3-4 minutes
MAKE AHEAD: you can prepare salad ingredients, dressing and marinade up to 24
hours ahead and chill; near serving time stirfry the squid, cool and assemble the salad

This salad has an intense chilli heat matched with a zingy freshness that is simply
irresistible. Chef Richard Harris cooks at Tribeca, my neighbourhood restaurant in
Auckland. I have adapted his recipe for the home kitchen.

500g / 1 lb baby squid tubes, each cut into 4-5 pieces
oil for frying

THAI MARINADE
1 tbsp oyster sauce
1 tbsp sweet soy sauce
2 tbsp fish sauce
1 large clove garlic, minced

GLASS NOODLE SALAD
50g / 2oz glass noodles (vermicelli)
3 spring (green) onions, sliced very finely on the diagonal
3 cups mixed fresh Asian herbs, torn (eg 1 cup each torn mint and
    coriander (cilantro) leaf, 1/2 cup each torn fresh basil and Vietnamese
    mint)
1 recipe Chilli Lime Dressing – see side panel
OPTIONAL: 1/2 cup crispy fried shallots (can be bought from
    most Asian food stores)
GARNISH: 1/2 cup roasted chopped peanuts, fresh lime wedges,
    chilli jam or 1/2-1 long, red fresh chilli, seeded and sliced very finely

CHILLI LIME DRESSING

2 tbsp freshly squeezed lime juice
2 tbsp fish sauce
1 1/2 tbsp sugar
1/4 -1/2 tsp crushed dried chilli flakes
(use more if desired)

Place dressing ingredients in a jar,
cover and shake thoroughly until
sugar has dissolved.

COMBINE marinade ingredients in a clean bowl with squid. Marinate 30 minutes then
drain. Heat 1 tablespoon oil in a heavy frypan until very hot and cook squid over high
heat in 3-4 batches for 45-60 seconds, just until it changes colour. Add extra oil to pan
between batches. Set squid aside and allow to cool completely.

POUR boiling water over noodles and leave to cool (they will hold for hours without
losing texture). Drain thoroughly, dry with paper towels and cut into shorter threads.

IN a mixing bowl combine drained noodles with spring onions, herbs, cooked squid
and enough dressing just to coat all ingredients. Mound salad into centre of serving
plates and sprinkle with crispy shallots if using. Scatter with chopped peanuts.

GARNISH with lime wedges and chilli jam or fresh chopped chilli. Serve immediately.

FOCACCIA WITH TOMATO, CAPER AND OLIVE TOPPING

MAKES: enough for 2 large loaves PREP TIME: 20 minutes plus about 1¼ hours rising COOK TIME: 20-25 minutes
MAKE AHEAD: prepared dough will keep covered in the fridge for up to 2 days where it will slowly rise, or can be frozen

There is something about a homemade loaf that speaks yards about home and hearth. Don't be tempted to keep adding flour – the dough should be very sticky and soft. This wetness ensures a much lighter bread. The dough can be frozen raw – let it rise then punch down, put in a clean plastic bag and freeze. It is an excellent pizza base and also makes the best breadsticks.

> 250g / 8oz potatoes, peeled and chopped
> or 1 packed cup mashed potato (can use leftover mash)
> 1½ cups warm (not hot) water
> 1½ tsp dry yeast
> ¼ cup extra virgin olive oil
> 2 tsp salt
> 4½-5 cups high-grade or all-purpose flour
> a little olive oil to knead
> TOPPING: ½ cup tasty olives, 2 tbsp capers, 1 tbsp chopped oregano,
> sprinkle of sea salt, 2 tbsp oil to drizzle

BOIL potatoes in lightly salted water until tender. Drain thoroughly, dry over heat in pan to evaporate excess water and mash until fine (don't use a food processor or potato will go gluey). Cool slightly then mix with warm water and yeast. (If using left-over mash, warm it a little in the microwave or mix with hot water before adding yeast). Stand for a couple of minutes to allow yeast to start working.

MIX in oil, salt and three-quarters of the flour until smooth, then roughly mix in remaining flour. Knead on an oiled bench about 20 times until dough comes together smoothly. It will be very sticky. Place in an oiled bowl, cover with plastic wrap and leave in a warm place until doubled in size (about 40 minutes) or refrigerate overnight to slowly rise.

DIVIDE dough into 2 and form each half into a flat, oblong loaf on lightly oiled trays. Leave to rise again in a warm place for 30 minutes or until dough is risen and puffy. Scatter topping ingredients over. Dimple the dough with your fingertips, sprinkle with a little salt and drizzle over oil. Bake at 220°C / 425°F for about 20 minutes or until golden and bread sounds hollow when tapped.

RIGHT: Focaccia with caperberries, hot smoked salmon and Horseradish Cream.

HORSERADISH CREAM

Sour cream takes well to a range of flavours. You can also combine it with mustard, dried onion soup powder or pesto for a simple dunking sauce.

Make horseradish cream by mixing 1 cup light sour cream with 2 tbsp horseradish sauce, 1 tbsp lemon juice and a little salt and pepper.

FETA DIP

This is nice to serve with focaccia or breadsticks.
Purée together 100g /4oz feta, 1 large clove garlic, 1 tsp capers, ⅓ cup water and ½ tsp fresh thyme or rosemary leaves. Makes 1⅓ cups. Dip will keep for several days, stored in a covered container in the fridge.

menu 4

LEEK, POTATO AND ROASTED GARLIC SOUP

POPPY SEED BREADSTICKS

Use the focaccia dough on page 42 to make these crunchy breadsticks.

Heat oven to 190°C / 375°F. After first rising divide dough in half on a floured board. Press out each half into a rectangle about 1cm / ½ inch thick and 14cm / 5 inches wide. Starting from narrow edge, cut finger-wide strips of dough, roll gently and rest a minute then stretch out to form long, thin snakes. Place on an oiled baking tray. Leave 10-15 minutes.

Brush breadsticks with water and sprinkle with seeds such as **poppy seeds, linseed, fennel seeds, sesame seeds or cornmeal.** Bake 15-20 minutes or until golden. Remove from oven.

Stir 1 tsp **salt** into ¼ cup **boiling water** to dissolve. Brush salted water over cooked breadsticks. Return to oven and bake at 150°C / 300°F for 10-15 minutes or until very crisp and crunchy.

Cool and store in an airtight container. Entire dough mixture makes about 50 breadsticks.

MAKES: about 7 cups, serves 6 PREP TIME: 10 minutes COOK TIME: 50 minutes
MAKE AHEAD: soup can be made up to 2-3 days ahead and chilled or frozen (in which case add roasted garlic and thyme when reheating from frozen)

This soup with its sweet, earthy flavour heralds the change of seasons and reminds me of the country and my friend and very good cook Jilly Jardine, digging leeks and picking fresh thyme in her lovely garden before the first really hard frosts hit. The air is cold enough to make your breath huff white and the leeks are crisp, fat and sweet. These early winter harvests offer pure, nourishing comfort in this robust and filling soup. If you want to turn it into more of a meal, place a slice of gruyère on top of each bowlful.

> 3 tbsp butter
> 2 large leeks, pale parts only, thinly sliced (save tops for stock)
> 3 medium potatoes, peeled and diced
> 4 cups good chicken stock
> 1 cup water
> 1 tsp salt
> 10-12 grinds black pepper
> 1 head or 10-12 cloves roasted garlic (page 97), drained of oil
> 1 tsp fresh thyme leaves (don't use dried; leave out if fresh
>   not available or substitute with oregano)
> OPTIONAL: 6 thin slices gruyère or cheddar to serve

IN a medium-large pot, heat butter and cook leeks over low heat for about 10 minutes, stirring now and then, until softened but not browned. Add potatoes, stock and water. Season with salt and pepper and bring to a simmer. Simmer 40 minutes. Add roasted garlic and thyme. Mash roughly with a potato masher (you could also purée but I prefer a chunkier texture). Serve hot topped with a slice of cheese if desired.

menu 9

44

ASSEMBLE

For people who don't do a lot of cooking or who live flat-out lives, creating fabulous food simply by assembling a few ingredients is a good option.

AVOCADOS WITH TOMATOES AND BALSAMIC DRESSING

Avocados, tomatoes and balsamic vinegar are very good company. The key is finding perfectly ripe avocados – if too ripe they have a foul taste. Cradle the fruit gently in your hand and feel if it gives a little, or press at the stem and see if it will push in.

PREPARE a recipe of Balsamic Dressing (page 22). Choose perfect, just-ripe avocados, allowing half per serve along with 2 cherry tomatoes. At serving time halve avocados and remove stones. Quarter cherry tomatoes and pile into avocado cavities, drizzle with Balsamic Dressing and serve.

ROASTED SCALLOPS IN THE HALF SHELL WITH LEMON OR LIME BUTTER

Dead simple and utterly delicious. Choose the freshest scallops. I like to remove the tough little hinge on the side of each one before cooking. Use other flavoured butters such as cumin or herb butter if preferred (see page 48).

PLACE fresh scallops in clean shells, dot each one with 1 teaspoon butter, a squeeze of lemon or lime juice and a grating of lemon or lime zest. Season with salt and pepper. Chill until ready to serve.

TO SERVE, place scallops under a hot grill for a couple of minutes until butter bubbles and scallop flesh turns opaque. Don't over-cook.

FRESH MELON AND PROSCIUTTO
A classic dish, beloved by the Italians. Ripe melon
should smell sweet and fruity.

PEEL and deseed a ripe melon and cut into wedges. Fold
paper-thin slices of prosciutto on top. Accompany with
lime wedges.

◇ ASPARAGUS AND HOLLANDAISE: Snap tough ends off
asparagus. Boil spears 3 minutes, drain and serve with lime
or lemon hollandaise (page 72).

◇ TOMATOES, BASIL AND FRESH MOZZARELLA: Slice ripe
vine tomatoes and layer with sliced fresh mozzarella.
Scatter with fresh basil leaves. Season with salt and ground
black pepper and drizzle with extra virgin olive oil.

SALMON CARPACCIO
Freshest salmon, sliced ultra thin with a very sharp knife,
offers an ultimate melt-in-the-mouth experience.
Flavouring the best extra virgin olive oil with a hint of
vanilla is something divine they do at Vinnies restaurant
in Auckland.

SLICE freshest, boneless, skinless salmon as thinly as
possible. Layer on a serving plate or place on bread.
Sprinkle with capers and finely grated lemon zest.
Season with salt and pepper and drizzle with a little
vanilla-flavoured olive oil.

◇ VANILLA-FLAVOURED OLIVE OIL: Mix 2 tablespoons of
the very best extra virgin olive oil with ¼ tsp vanilla
extract.

DUCK AND MANGO SALAD

SERVES: 8 PREP TIME: 20 minutes COOK TIME: 10 minutes (to crisp duck skin)
MAKE AHEAD: prepare all ingredients ready for assembly and chill up to 8 hours before serving; combine dressing ingredients in a jar and chill up to 2 days

Asian supermarkets frequently sell hot roasted ducks. They are delicious, though often quite fatty. Regardless of when you plan to use the meat, strip it off the bone and remove skin before chilling. Any visible fat can be easily removed at the same time. If you can't get roasted duck, make this with roasted chicken instead.

1 roasted duck
20-30 snow peas
2 large ripe mangos, peeled and flesh chopped or
     425g / 15oz can mangos in juice, drained and chopped
2 spring (green) onions, finely sliced
1/2 cup chopped mint or coriander (cilantro) leaves or a mixture of both
2 cups fresh mung bean sprouts
OPTIONAL: 300g / 11oz udon noodles, cooked

GINGER
SESAME
DRESSING

1/4 cup lime or lemon juice
1 tsp fish sauce
1 tsp brown sugar
1 tsp sesame oil
1 tsp minced fresh ginger
2 tbsp flavourless oil eg grapeseed
1 tbsp rice vinegar
1 tbsp soy sauce
1 small red chilli, seeded and finely chopped
salt and freshly ground black pepper

REMOVE duck skin and place on a baking tray. Grill or roast until crispy. Drain off all fat and cut crisp skin into thin strips or coarsely crumble. Set aside.

SHRED duck meat, discarding fat and bones. Pour boiling water over snow peas then cool at once under cold water. Drain then slice thinly on an angle. Place in a mixing bowl with all other salad ingredients. Cover and chill until ready to serve.

COMBINE dressing ingredients and toss through salad. Serve at once.

DUCK KNOW-HOW

Roasted duck meat can be frozen. Use the carcass as the base for a noodle soup, adding chicken stock to cover and flavouring with a little orange zest, fresh ginger, chopped spring (green) onions, a few whole star anise and a splash of soy sauce. Simmer for 1/2 hour then strain and add noodles and any fresh greens of your choice.

FLAVOURED BUTTERS

These are useful for adding flavour and an unctuous note to seafood, chicken, duck and beef or for serving with bread.

SPICY CUMIN BUTTER

Mix 4 tbsp butter with 1 tsp ground cumin seeds, 1/2 tsp chilli powder and the finely grated zest of 1/2 lemon.

HERB BUTTER

Mix 4 tbsp butter with 2 tbsp chopped fresh soft herbs such as tarragon, chervil, basil or parsley.

ROASTING

Roasting is one of the easiest ways to cook. There's no standing over a hot stove, consulting procedures, wondering if you are doing the right thing – you simply put the food in a hot oven, put the timer on and go and have a hot bath or a walk in the garden with a nice cold gin, leaving the oven and its dry, caramelising heat to do its thing. And the results are so satisfying – roast chicken must be the world's favourite dish.

The most taxing part of cooking a roast is figuring out the timing for accompaniments and getting everything out on the table at the same time, with nothing cold or overcooked. If you serve just a salad as a side dish, you won't find a simpler meal that offers more rewards. Beyond the satisfactions of sweet flavours and juicy textures that roasting delivers, lies a central spirit of generosity that nourishes our sense of tradition.

If you are serving a full-on roast with all the trimmings – roast and boiled vegetables, stuffing and sauce – a bit of a last-minute dance is required kitchenside. Plan your timing around what takes longest (usually the meat) and work back. Roast vegetables will usually go into the oven about 45 minutes before the meat is ready. When everything is cooked, and the meat comes out to rest, the oven temperature gets fired up to brown and crisp roast vegetables. Make or heat a sauce, cook some fresh green vegetables and thoroughly warm serving plates.

Neurotic worrying that food will get cold has us rushing everything to the table the minute it comes out of the oven and before the meat has had time to rest. Resting meat is critical to the cooking process – it ensures tenderness, even colour and moisture retention. The bigger the cut the longer the time it needs to sit. A steak will need a good 3-4 minutes, a beef fillet 10-15 minutes and a leg of lamb a good 15-20 minutes resting before it is carved. Cover with a piece of foil, put a couple of towels on top and leave it in a warm place. At serving time it will be tender, moist and juicy.

LEFT: Lemon Roast Chicken served with Apricot and Pine Nut Stuffing (recipes pages 68 and 69)

ROAST LEG OF LAMB

SERVES: 6 PREP TIME: 10 minutes COOK TIME: 1-1½ hours
MAKE AHEAD: prepare lamb ready for roasting up to 12 hours ahead

Ask your butcher to take the femur bone out of a leg of lamb – this produces a carvery roast that is very easy to slice for serving. Anchovies give the lamb a real richness and depth of flavour and, even though you use a lot here, there's certainly no fishiness. I particularly like this combination of anchovies and rosemary, which comes from the kitchens of Italy. Sliced cloves of garlic are another popular addition, either with the rosemary or the anchovies. Here the lamb is roasted hot and fast to produce a lightly rare result. It can also be slow roasted for more of a fall-apart texture, in which case cook for 3½-4 hours at 150°C / 300°F in a covered roasting dish.

> 1.3-1.5kg / 3½-4½ lb leg of lamb (carvery roast)
> 8-10 anchovies, halved lengthways
> about 16 tiny sprigs rosemary
> juice of 1 lemon
> salt and freshly ground black pepper

REDCURRANT 1½ tbsp redcurrant or quince jelly
JUS
2 cups beef or vegetable stock
1 tsp balsamic vinegar
1 tbsp cornflour (cornstarch) mixed with ¼ cup Marsala or tawny port
salt to taste

USE a sharp, thin-bladed knife to make 16-20 narrow, deep cuts all over the lamb. Into each hole stuff half an anchovy fillet (if anchovies are mushy just grab a ½ tsp mound and stuff it deep into each hole). Insert sprigs of rosemary in holes and squeeze over lemon juice. Chill until ready to cook.

HEAT oven to 180°C / 350°F. Place lamb in a roasting pan and season with salt and pepper. Roast 1-1¼ hours or until cooked to your liking (it is nicest served slightly rare). Remove meat from oven, cover to keep warm and rest for 10 minutes.

WHILE meat rests, make sauce (jus). Drain off any excess fat and place roasting pan over direct heat. Add jelly, stock and vinegar and stir well to release pan brownings. Simmer and thicken with cornflour and marsala mixture. Season to taste. If desired whisk in a small knob of butter just before serving. If it tastes a bit bland you can add a squeeze of lemon juice or a teaspoon of miso – this adds a real boost of flavour.

ACCOMPANY lamb with roast vegetables such as crispy potatoes, beetroot (beets) and onions, and jus. For a simpler meal serve with roasted vegetables brought to room temperature and tossed with salad greens.

MOROCCAN ROAST LAMB

Rub meat all over with **lemon juice**, sprinkle liberally with commercial **Moroccan spice** and season with **salt and pepper**. Chill up to 48 hours before roasting to allow flavours to infuse. Accompany with **Roasted Tomato Sauce** (page 96).

NORTH INDIAN CARDAMOM AND CHILLI ROAST LAMB

Mix 1 cup **yogurt** with 2 cloves crushed **garlic**, 1 tsp **cardamom seeds**, roughly crushed, 1 tsp **chilli powder**, 2 tsp **garam masala**, juice of ½ **lemon**, ½ tsp **turmeric powder**, 1 tsp **salt** and ½ tsp finely ground **black pepper**.

Make small slashes in a whole bone-in lamb leg in several places. Spread marinade into all the openings. Chill up to 48 hours before roasting to allow flavours to infuse. Slow roast with marinade at 150°C / 300°F in a covered dish for 3½-4 hours, uncovering in last ½ hour.

PERFECT ROAST BEEF WITH SHALLOT SAUCE

SERVES: 6 PREP TIME: 10 minutes plus at least 1 hour marinating
COOK TIME: 20-25 minutes
MAKE AHEAD: marinate meat up to 48 hours ahead; brown meat and chill and make sauce up to 24 hours before serving

I find beef fillet immensely gratifying to cook – it does not mind waiting around, is a happy chameleon to a vast array of sauces and flavourings and, provided you don't overcook it, tastes superb hot or cold. Here I have used a simple balsamic and horseradish marinade but you can keep the meat plain if preferred.

800g-1kg / 2 lb piece beef fillet (tenderloin)
1 tbsp balsamic vinegar
2 tsp horseradish sauce or Dijon mustard
salt and freshly ground black pepper
spritz of oil to brown meat

SHALLOT
SAUCE
1 tsp butter
2 shallots, finely diced
1 tbsp fish sauce
1 cup red wine
2 cups beef stock
salt and ground black pepper

TIE fillet into a neat roll with cooking string. Mix balsamic vinegar and horseradish and rub all over meat. Cover and marinate at least 1 hour or up to 48 hours in the fridge.

SEASON meat with salt and pepper and brown all over in a hot, lightly oiled pan. Transfer to a baking tray lined with parchment. Use the unwashed pan to make the sauce.

TO COOK BEEF: Heat oven to 180°C / 350°F and roast beef 20-25 minutes or until cooked to your liking. Take from oven, cover and rest at least 10 minutes before serving in thick slices with sauce.

TO PREPARE SHALLOT SAUCE: Heat butter over low heat in the frypan used to brown the meat. Add shallot and gently sizzle 5 minutes or until shallot is softened but not browned. Add fish sauce, wine and stock and simmer 5 minutes, stirring to lift pan brownings. Season with salt and pepper. Strain, discarding solids. Chill sauce if not using within a couple of hours.

LEFT: Perfect Roast Beef with Shallot Sauce,
Wilted Spinach (page 91) and Mash (page 90), garnished with Parsnip Crisps (page 64).

TESTING FOR DONENESS

Raw meat feels very squidgy, like the flesh at the base of your palm. Press the meat with your finger in the thickest part and gauge the amount of resistance. Rare meat will feel spongy with a slight resistance. Medium rare, which is how we often like it, is semi-squidgy. Touch your thumb to your middle finger and feel the texture at the base of your palm – this is the closest comparison. Medium cooked meat will feel slightly firm and springy to the touch. Well-done meat is very springy and bounces back quickly.
For best results meat should be at room temperature before cooking.

CARVING MEAT

To ensure maximum tenderness, always carve meat across the grain.

DINNER IN A FLASH

Now for some simple, smart dinners for last-minute invites, impromptu arrivals and harried schedules.

CAJUN ROAST FISH FOR TWO

Coat fish in a spice mix and roast in a hot oven for 5-6 minutes to serve with salad or vegetables. You can use all kinds of spice mixes. Here I've chosen a good commercial cajun blend.

Heat oven to 250°C / 500°F. Place 2 red capsicums (bell peppers) quartered lengthways, seeds and pith removed, in a roasting dish. Season with salt and pepper and drizzle with a little olive oil. Bake 15 minutes. Dip 4 fillets of dense, boneless, skinless fresh fish into 2 tbsp extra virgin olive oil to coat. Sprinkle 1 tsp commercial Cajun spice mix over each fillet. Season with salt and pepper. Place in oven with capsicums for 6-8 minutes or until cooked through. Place on serving plate. Squeeze over the juice of a lime or lemon. Accompany with roast potatoes.

THAI BEEF AND NOODLE SALAD FOR FOUR

You can use cooked beef at room temperature, or cook a thick steak to medium rare and leave to cool.

Combine ¼ cup lime or lemon juice, 1 tbsp fish sauce, ¼ cup sweet Thai chilli sauce, 1 tsp sesame oil and 1 red chilli, finely diced (optional), to make a dressing. Thinly slice 400-600g / about 1 lb rare cooked beef and mix with dressing. Toss together 1 large cucumber (eg telegraph) cut into 6cm / 2 inch lengths and each piece cut into batons, 2 red capsicums (bell peppers), thinly sliced, 4 spring (green) onions, thinly sliced, 4 medium-large tomatoes, cut in thin segments, 20 blanched snow peas, ¼ cup chopped mint leaves and ¼ cup toasted peanuts (optional). Just before serving, mix in 150g / 5oz crispy (Chinese) noodles. (To blanch snow peas, drop in boiling water, drain and cool.)

GLAZED CHILLI LIME CHICKEN FOR FOUR

This makes a fabulous whip together dinner that tastes like you have gone to a lot of trouble. Serve with rice and veg.

Place 4-5 chicken Marylands or 2 large halved poussins, skin side up in a single layer, in a large, shallow baking dish. Mix ½ cup sweet Thai chilli sauce, ¼ cup water, 1 tbsp fish sauce, 1 tbsp soy sauce, and the juice of ½ lime and pour over chicken. Season with salt and pepper and bake 25-30 minutes in a 200°C / 400°F oven, or until juices run clear. Accompany with rice and stirfried snow peas.

◇ GLAZED CHILLI LIME SALMON

Prepare recipe using 4-5 salmon steaks and omitting water. Bake at 220°C / 425°F for 7-8 minutes until just cooked.

SALSA VERDE FOR ANYTIME

A useful green sauce to have on hand as a summer fridge staple. It's terrific with any red meat, chicken or fish and keeps for several weeks in the fridge.

Purée until smooth 1½ packed cups parsley leaves, ½ packed cup mint leaves, 1 small handful chives, chopped, 1 cup extra virgin olive oil, 3 tbsp capers, 3 cloves garlic, 2 tsp Dijon mustard, ¼ small red onion, chopped, and 4-5 anchovies. Store in the fridge. Makes about 1½ cups. Here a thick slice of rare roasted beef is served on a bed of lightly cooked sliced capsicums (bell peppers) and beans with salsa verde spooned on top. Roasted potatoes would be a good accompaniment.

MINT ROASTED LAMB RACKS WITH BEETROOT AND ONIONS

SERVES: 6 PREP TIME: 10 minutes COOK TIME: 50 minutes
MAKE AHEAD: make sauce up to a week ahead; brown meat up to 24 hours ahead

Lamb racks fall into the category of low effort high performance food – there's very little required to produce an utterly pleasing result. You can use this treatment with other lamb cuts – thick-cut leg steaks or rumps, for example. Well ahead of time you can roll the lamb in mint and sear to brown. Make the sauce ahead of time and have the vegetables prepared ready to cook.

> 4 racks lamb, trimmed (allow 3-4 cutlets per serve)
> salt and ground black pepper
> 2 tbsp chopped fresh mint
> a little oil to brown
> 6 whole, unpeeled onions
> 6 whole, unpeeled beetroot (beets)
> 1 tbsp maple syrup or honey
> TO SERVE: **Sweet and Sour Mustard Seed Sauce (page 97)**

SEASON meat with salt and pepper and roll in mint to coat. Spray a little oil into a heavy pan set over a high heat and sear meat about 3 minutes or until well browned all over. Cool, cover and put to one side or chill if not cooking at once.

HEAT oven to 180°C / 350°F. Place onions and beetroot in a roasting dish. Rub with a little oil and season with salt and pepper. Drizzle a spoonful of maple syrup or honey over the beetroot. Roast 40 minutes or until tender, turning occasionally.

PLACE meat on a roasting tray, allowing space between racks so they can cook evenly. Bake 12-15 minutes or until done to your liking. Cover and rest 5 minutes before carving.

TO SERVE: Place 2-3 cutlets per person on a bed of Minted Shoestring Zucchini (see side panel). Accompany with roasted beetroot and onions and Sweet and Sour Mustard Seed Sauce (page 97). Pass bowls of green vegetables and roasted potatoes.

MINTED SHOESTRING ZUCCHINI

3-4 **zucchini**, cut in matchstick strips (a mandolin or Benriner slicer makes fast work of this), 6-8 **mint leaves**, finely chopped, 1 tbsp **olive oil**, 2 tbsp **water**, ½ tsp salt, several grinds **black pepper** and the finely grated zest of ½ **lemon**.

Prepare zucchini and mint, cover and chill until ready to cook. Place in a heavy pan with oil, water, salt, pepper and zest. Stirfry over a high heat 2-3 minutes or until just wilted. Serve at once.
MAKE AHEAD: Slice zucchini up to 8 hours ahead and chill.

WARM PLATES

Cold plates are the fastest way to cool a hot meal. Heated plates make all the difference to keeping food hot. To warm a stack of dinner plates in a hurry, rinse them under water, drain off excess and place in a microwave.
A stack of 4-6 plates will heat through in about 5 minutes.
Dry off before using.

GRILLED GREEK CHEESE AND ROASTED VEGETABLE SALAD WITH LAMB

SERVES: 4-6 PREP TIME: 10 minutes COOK TIME: 25 minutes
MAKE AHEAD: everything can be prepared and cooked ahead of time ready to assemble

Roasted vegetables have a dense, rich succulence. Here they are partnered with grilled cheese, cherry tomatoes and beans. With a couple of slices of roasted lamb rack on top this makes a light, satisfying, summer meal. Don't do what I did when I prepared the salad for the photo and forget to add the dressing!

200g / 7oz feta, haloumi or sheep's cheese, cut into chunks
1 red and 1 yellow capsicum (bell pepper), seeds and pith removed,
    flesh chopped into 3cm / 1 inch chunks
2-3 zucchini, angle sliced into 1.5cm / ½ inch pieces
2 tbsp olive oil
1 clove garlic, peeled and crushed
salt and freshly ground pepper
300g / 11oz green beans
OPTIONAL: 2 roasted lamb racks (page 58) or 300g / 10oz
    cooked lamb
12-16 cherry tomatoes
½ cup tasty black olives
1 recipe Greek Olive Dressing – see side panel
TO SERVE: 300g / 11oz baby spinach or mixed salad leaves

GRILL feta on a baking tray about 5 minutes or until browned on one side. Cool on tray until firm enough to handle.

TO ROAST vegetables, heat oven to 220°C / 425°F. Place capsicums and zucchini in a roasting dish. Mix through oil and garlic and season with salt and pepper. Roast about 15 minutes or until tender and lightly browned. Cool on tray.

BOIL beans in lightly salted water for 3 minutes. Refresh under cold water and drain.

ROAST lamb as per page 58 or, if using cooked lamb, warm it in a microwave for 2 minutes to soften or wrap in foil and warm in a hot oven for 6-8 minutes just before serving.

TO SERVE: place grilled feta, roasted vegetables, beans, tomatoes and olives in a mixing bowl. Pour over dressing and gently toss to combine. Pile spinach leaves onto plates and top with salad and warm lamb.

GREEK OLIVE DRESSING

2 tbsp olive oil, ¼ cup lemon juice, 1 tbsp chopped mint and oregano, 6 salty black olives, pitted and chopped, ½ tsp salt and several grinds black pepper. Shake all ingredients together in a screw-top jar. Dressing will keep a week in the fridge.

CHILLI MINT SALSA

This simple combination is wonderful with lamb. If you choose to use it in the salad opposite instead of the Greek Olive Dressing, then leave out the grilled cheese.

Combine 2 tbsp sugar, 2 tbsp oil, 2 tbsp rice vinegar, finely grated zest and juice of 1 lime, 1 tbsp fish sauce and 1 red chilli, finely minced. Chill until ready to serve (up to 24 hours ahead). At serving time pour boiling water over about 40 mint leaves, drain immediately and refresh under cold water. Chop and mix into salsa with 2 finely chopped spring (green) onions.

PARTNERS FOR A ROAST

• Green salad, roast potatoes and roasted red and yellow capsciums (bell peppers)

• Kumara (sweet potato) mash, green beans and Sweet and Sour Mustard Seed Sauce

• Roast vegetable platter, cooked beans, asparagus and broccoli, Redcurrant Jus

• Mash, wilted spinach, Pop Tarts, parsnip crisps, shallot sauce

• Warm roast vegetables tossed with salad greens, Roast Garlic Aioli

• Roasted sweet capsicums (bell peppers), roast potatoes and tossed green salad

• Peas and beans, roast vegetables and Red Onion Riesling Gravy

BAKED KUMARA

Allow 1 medium-sized fresh (preferably organic) kumara (sweet potato) per person. Scrub and prick skin in several places. Bake at 180°C / 350°F for about 1 hour or until tender. Split in half to serve.

menu 6

CRACKLING APPLE ROAST PORK WITH BALSAMIC ONIONS

SERVES: 8-10 PREP TIME: 20 minutes, plus marinating COOK TIME: about 3 hours
MAKE AHEAD: pork can be prepared ready to roast up to 24 hours ahead

You will need to ask a butcher to prepare the roast with extra skin attached, or else buy a separate piece of belly skin to roll the pork in. Also ask the butcher to score the skin. Rolling apple inside gives the pork a lovely sweet flavour but is not essential.

> 1 whole skin on pork scotch fillet (rib eye – loin cut from the neck end) about 1.5kg / 3$\frac{1}{2}$ lb with extra 30cm / 12 inches extra skin cut from shoulder to wrap around pork fully, excess fat trimmed off
> 1 tbsp fennel seeds, lightly toasted and finely ground
> salt and freshly ground black pepper
> OPTIONAL: 1 cup cooked apple slices
> a little oil to rub over skin
> 2 red onions, peeled and cut in thin wedges
> 1 head fresh fennel, thinly sliced (or use an extra onion)
> 2 cups white wine or chicken stock
> 1 tbsp balsamic vinegar
> 1 tbsp brown sugar
> 6 whole small apples, preferably tart flavour
> 1 tbsp cornflour (cornstarch) mixed with 2 tbsp water

LAY pork on bench, skin side down. Sprinkle meat with half the ground fennel and season with salt and pepper. Place apple slices on top of meat then roll up to fully enclose with the skin. Secure with kitchen string at 2cm / 1 inch intervals. Rub pork skin with a little oil then rub in remaining fennel seed and some salt. Cover and chill for up to 24 hours.

HEAT oven to 220°C / 425°F. Place onions and fennel in a large baking dish with wine, balsamic vinegar and sugar and put pork on top. Bake about 45 minutes or until skin starts to bubble. Reduce heat to 160°C / 325°F. Run a sharp knife around the equator of the apples to cut through the skin and place them around the pork.

COOK a further 1$\frac{3}{4}$-2 hours or until pork reaches an internal temperature of 70°C / 160°F, or when the juices run clear when skewered. Add an extra cup of water to roasting pan if needed. Remove meat and apples from dish, cover and set aside about 10 minutes in a warm place. Skim off any fat from dish. Add cornflour mixture to vegetable juices and stir over heat until lightly thickened. Serve pork with roasted apple and thickened juices. Baked kumara make a nice accompaniment.

RIGHT: Crackling Apple Roast Pork with peas and baked kumara.

ON THE SIDE

Starchy side dishes round out a meal and make us feel satisfied. As well as these options mash, couscous, pasta, rice and beans will also fit the bill.

PARSNIP CRISPS

Crunchy parsnips make a fabulous side dish or garnish. They can be made in bulk and stored in an airtight container for up to a week. When required pop them into a paper bag and put in a hot oven for 10-15 minutes to recrisp. Other vegetables such as beetroot or kumara (sweet potatoes) can also be used.

Use a mandolin, peeler or grater to cut shavings of 2-3 peeled and trimmed parsnips. Place in a large roasting pan and mix through 2-3 tbsp cup olive oil. Roast at 180°C / 350°F for about 30 minutes or until golden and crisp, stirring about every 10 minutes. Reheat as required. Serves 8. Parsnip shavings can also be deep-fried in hot oil until crisp and reheated in the oven at serving time.

THYME ROASTED BABY POTATOES

Choose a floury potato for best results and allow 4-5 small potatoes per serve.

Wash potatoes well or peel if preferred. Place in a saucepan, cover with cold water and add 1 teaspoon salt. Bring to the boil then turn off heat and leave to cool. Drain thoroughly and chill until ready to roast. Place in an ovenproof dish with 2 tbsp olive oil and 1-2 sprigs fresh thyme, rosemary or oregano. Toss potatoes to coat in oil. Season with salt and pepper. Roast at 220°C / 425°F for about 35 minutes or until golden.

POP TARTS

Aka Yorkshire pudding, which is traditionally served with roast beef and gravy, but made in muffin pans. These are perfectly named as they do just irresistibly pop into your mouth. You can also mix fresh herbs or roasted vegetables or cheese into the batter before cooking.

Whisk together ½ cup milk, 2 eggs, ¾ cup flour and ½ tsp salt until smooth. Stand 10 minutes then whisk in ½ cup cold water.
Heat oven to 200°C / 400°F. Drop ½ teaspoon oil into each pan of a 12-pan medium muffin tray. Place tray in oven for 5 minutes. Pour 2 tbsp batter into each hot, oiled pan. Bake 15-20 minutes or until puffed and golden. Serve immediately. Makes 12 pop tarts.

GOATS' CHEESE POTATO ROSTI

When you cook rosti in a frypan they tend to absorb a lot of oil and take ages to cook. Forming them into shapes then baking them takes out a lot of stove work.

Peel and grate 700g / 1½ lb floury potatoes into a bowl of cold water. Drain and squeeze dry. Place in a mixing bowl, season with salt and pepper and mix through 150g / 5oz crumbled goats' cheese and 2 tbsp chopped parsley. Place a 10cm / 4 inch round cutter or egg poaching mould on a baking tray, fill with potato mixture and pack down firmly. Repeat to make 8 cakes. Brush with olive oil and bake at 200°C / 400°F for 40 minutes or until crisp and golden. Alternatively, panfry cakes in a little oil.

PROSCIUTTO-WRAPPED CHICKEN WITH SOUTHERN ITALIAN VEGETABLE SAUCE

SERVES: 6 PREP TIME: 12-15 minutes COOK TIME: 20 minutes
MAKE AHEAD: wrap chicken ready to bake and make sauce up to 24 hours ahead

It's amazing how a couple of sage leaves and a slice of prosciutto can transform a chicken breast into something that tastes really special. The same treatment is equally successful with pork fillets. The pretty, vibrant sauce that accompanies the chicken is useful to add to your sauce repertoire – either to partner grilled steaks or in pasta dishes. However you choose to flavour chicken breasts – be it with bacon, a flavoured butter pushed under the skin or with a spicy Moroccan marinade – you'll find that twenty minutes in a hot oven delivers perfectly cooked, moist, tender breasts. Don't forget to cover and rest in a warm place for 6-8 minutes before serving.

SOFT POLENTA

I put soft polenta in the category of comfort food – there's something very calming about its soft, creamy simplicity. You can jazz up the basic recipe with blue cheese or roasted garlic or any other flavourings that take your fancy. The thing to remember is that once the polenta has cooked you can't cool and reheat it because it sets solid. While this is useful if you want to make polenta wedges (see page 76), it means that if you like it soft you need to cook it at the last minute.

6 cups water
1 tsp salt
freshly ground pepper
1 1/2 cups instant polenta
1/4 cup grated parmesan
1 tbsp butter

Bring water, salt and pepper to the boil in a saucepan. Add polenta in a thin stream as you stir. Cover and cook 3 minutes. Stir in parmesan and butter.

12 sage leaves
6 boneless chicken breasts, preferably organic
6 slices prosciutto or 6-8 slices streaky bacon

SOUTHERN ITALIAN VEGETABLE SAUCE

2 tbsp olive oil
1 sprig rosemary leaves, finely chopped
2 smallish zucchini, finely chopped
2 red capsicums (bell peppers), finely chopped
1 onion, finely chopped
3 cloves garlic, crushed
400g / 14oz can tomatoes, puréed (1 1/2 cups)
1 tsp brown sugar
1 tsp white wine vinegar
salt and pepper to taste
OPTIONAL: 1/2 cup small black Italian olives eg Gaeta olives
TO SERVE: 1 recipe soft polenta - see side panel
TO GARNISH: fresh sage leaves

COMBINE sauce ingredients and simmer gently until cooked, about 8-10 minutes. Check seasonings and adjust to taste. Chill until ready to serve.

PLACE a couple of sage leaves on top of each chicken breast and wrap with prosciutto to enclose. Chill until ready to cook.

HEAT oven to 200°C / 400°F. Season chicken with salt and pepper. Place on a baking tray lined with baking parchment and bake 20 minutes or until juices run clear.

TO SERVE: spoon soft polenta into serving bowls or plates. Top with warmed sauce. Angle slice each breast and arrange on top of sauce. Garnish with a little fresh sage.

ADDING FLAVOUR
TO ROAST CHICKEN

Stuff flavoured herb butters
(page 48) or **goats' cheese** and
herbs under the breast skin
before roasting.
If you are in a hurry simply stuff
a lemon in the chicken cavity
and slather a bit of butter over
the breast.

BRINING CHICKEN

There's a fashion among American
chefs of brining chicken and pork
before cooking to add moisture
and flavour to the meat, rather
than simply seasoning the skin.
Place 1 cup fine **salt** in a bowl
that will hold the chicken. Add
water to cover and stir to dissolve.
Add more water if needed to fully
cover bird. Chill for 1 hour then
drain and dry before roasting.

TENDER LEEKS

When leeks are young you can
eat the entire plant. Otherwise
just use the white base and pale
end of stalks.
To achieve melting tenderness
in leeks, slice and place in a pot
with 2 tbsp **olive oil** and 1 cup
chicken stock. Season and simmer
for 12-15 minutes or until tender.

FAVOURITE ROAST CHICKEN

There's a huge and universal satisfaction factor in roast chicken, and it's so easy to prepare. Start with a premium, quality bird – organic preferably or at least free range – and you will find the flavour difference immeasurable. Your average store-bought chicken takes about an hour to roast. Add an extra 15 minutes for an organic bird as the flesh is notably denser. On the side serve stuffing, old-fashioned bread sauce, roast vegetables and freshly cooked greens.

LEMON ROAST CHICKEN WITH RED ONION AND RIESLING GRAVY

SERVES: 4-6 PREP TIME: 15 minutes COOK TIME: about 1½ hours
MAKE AHEAD: prepare chicken and vegetables ready for roasting up to 4 hours ahead (keep chicken chilled)

1 large, whole chicken (preferably organic) about 1.5kg / 3 lb,
    visible fat removed
2 tbsp melted butter
1 juicy lemon, halved
salt and ground black pepper
1 clove garlic, crushed
1 tsp thyme leaves

RED ONION   6-8 smallish red onions, peeled and halved
RIESLING   1½ cups riesling
GRAVY   1- 1½ cups chicken stock
             1 tbsp cornflour (cornstarch) mixed with 2 tbsp water

HEAT oven to 220°C / 425°F. Dry chicken inside and out with paper towels. Place breast side up in a deep oven dish that has been brushed or sprayed with a little olive oil. Brush melted butter over chicken, squeeze over lemon juice, season with salt and pepper and sprinkle with garlic and thyme. Place squeezed lemon halves in chicken cavity. Arrange onions, cut side down, around bird.

ROAST 20-30 minutes or until chicken starts to brown. Add riesling and 1 cup stock to dish and cook a further 45-60 minutes, brushing chicken with pan liquids a couple of times. Cook until juices run clear when bird is pricked in the densest part or until meat temperature reaches 82°C / 180°F (place thermometer deep into the thigh).

TRANSFER chicken to a serving platter and keep warm. Stir cornflour mixture into pan juices over heat, adding extra ½ cup stock or vegetable water if required. Simmer 2-3 minutes. Season to taste and serve with chicken.

BREAD SAUCE

This is an old-fashioned, comforting alternative to stuffing that's very simple to prepare.

◇ 1 onion, finely diced ◇ 2¹/₂ cups milk
◇ 4 thick, crustless slices stale bread
◇ ¹/₄ tsp salt ◇ shake of white pepper
◇ 1 tsp fresh thyme leaves ◇ ¹/₄ tsp freshly grated nutmeg

Simmer onion in milk over low heat for 10 minutes. Add bread, broken into chunks. Season with salt, pepper and thyme. Simmer gently, stirring occasionally, for 5 minutes. Put into a serving dish and sprinkle with nutmeg.

APRICOT AND PINE NUT STUFFING

This stuffing works well with chicken, turkey and pork.

◇ 3 tbsp butter ◇ 1 large onion, finely diced ◇ ¹/₂ cup dried apricots, chopped
◇ 2 tsp chopped fresh thyme ◇ ¹/₄ cup pine nuts, toasted ◇ 2 tbsp finely chopped parsley ◇ 2-2¹/₂ cups fresh breadcrumbs
◇ 1 large egg ◇ salt and ground black pepper ◇ 2 slices bacon, diced and crispy fried (optional)

Heat butter in a frypan and cook onion over gentle heat for 5 minutes or until clear. Remove from heat and mix in other ingredients. Stuff into bird cavity. Alternatively, arrange in a thick sausage shape on baking parchment or oiled foil and roll tightly. Bake in the oven with chicken for about 40 minutes.

TWICE-ROASTED FIVE SPICE DUCK ON NOODLES AND BOK CHOY

SERVES: 6-8 PREP TIME: 10 minutes plus marinating for at least 1 hour COOK
TIME: 1 hour 40 minutes
MAKE AHEAD: marinate duck up to 24 hours ahead; roast to end of first stage
up to 8 hours before serving

I often order duck when I eat out – it's my all-time favourite meat. It can be tricky to
cook with stringy flesh or too much fat, however this method delivers excellent results
– a blast of hot heat to release fat then a slow braise to render the flesh juicy and moist
and the skin crispy.

> 2 large ducks or 8 duck quarters, preferably leg or thigh
> 1 recipe Five Spice Rub – see side panel
> 1 tsp salt (or to taste)
> 3-4 whole star anise
> 2 tbsp lemon juice
> 1 cup strained orange juice
> 2 cups chicken stock
> 1 tbsp soy sauce mixed with 1 tsp cornflour (cornstarch)
> salt and ground black pepper
> TO SERVE: 400g cooked fresh egg noodles and 6 heads bok choy
> or other Asian greens – see side panel

CUT whole ducks into quarters, cutting through the backbone (you can get the butcher
to do this). Prick skin all over with a sharp skewer (to release fat during cooking).
Rub five spice mixture over skin and flesh. Leave to marinate in fridge for up to 48
hours.

HEAT oven to 220°C / 425°F. Season duck with salt, place on a roasting rack and bake
40 minutes. Remove from oven and drain off fat. (Cool and chill if not using at once.)

REDUCE oven heat to 170°C / 340°F. Remove roasting rack, return duck to roasting
pan with star anise, lemon and orange juice and 1 cup stock. Cook a further 50-60
minutes. In last 10-15 minutes increase oven temperature to 220°C / 425°F to crisp
the skin if desired.

TO FINISH sauce, lift duck out of pan and keep warm. Remove any fat that has
accumulated on top of cooking liquid. Add remaining stock to pan and mix in soy and
cornflour mixture. Stir over heat until lightly thickened. Adjust seasonings to taste.

TO SERVE: divide noodles between serving bowls, top with greens and duck and ladle
over sauce.

BOK CHOY

Bok choy has a high water content and, like cabbage, needs to be cooked at the
last minute.

Allow 1 head baby bok choy per serve. Cut each one into quarters lengthwise and wash
well. Heat 1 tbsp sesame oil in a wok or pan. Add wet bok choy and a grating of fresh ginger.
Cover and cook over high heat for 2-3 minutes or until wilted, stirring
occasionally. Serve at once.
For other dense greens such as gai larn, broccoli or beans, follow the same method, adding ¼ cup
water to the pan and increasing the cooking time to 5-6 minutes.

FIVE SPICE RUB

Combine the finely grated zest of 2 lemons (no pith) with 1 tbsp five spice powder and
freshly ground black pepper.

EASY LIME HOLLANDAISE

This is made in a flash in a food processor. Use lemons if pre-ferred.

3 fresh egg yolks, at room temperature
2 tbsp lime juice
1/2 tsp salt
several grinds black pepper
100g / 1/2 cup butter

Blitz yolks, lime juice, salt and pepper in a food processor or blender. Heat butter until bubbling but not browned (it needs to be very hot for the sauce to fully thicken). With motor running, gradually add hot butter to egg mixture in a slow stream. Chill if not using within a couple of hours.

If sauce has been chilled, reheat with care as it will curdle if overheated. I find the best way to do this is to sit a bowl of sauce inside a bowl of hot water for a minute or two.

FLASH-ROASTED CHERRY TOMATOES

Allow 2-3 tomatoes with stems on per serve. Place on a roasting tray and bake at 200-250°C / 400-475°F for 3-5 minutes or until they just start to soften.

MEDITERRANEAN STUFFED SALMON FILLETS WITH LIME HOLLANDAISE

SERVES: 6-8 (filling can be extended as required) PREP TIME: 10 minutes
COOK TIME: 6-8 minutes
MAKE AHEAD: salmon can be stuffed up to 12 hours ahead if kept well chilled

Fresh salmon fillets offer scope for numerous quick and glamorous transformations that can be prepared ahead ready for a quick flash in the oven at serving time. Here the simple pine nut stuffing transforms the fish into something that looks and tastes as if you have gone to vast effort. If I am serving a first course I put the fish in the oven to cook for 5 minutes while I am setting up the appetiser and give it another 2-3 minute burst to heat through and finish cooking while I am setting out the main course.

6 x 150g / 5oz boneless, skinless salmon fillets, cut from the thick end
salt and freshly ground black pepper
juice of 1/2 lemon

STUFFING   1/4 cup finely chopped Italian parsley
1/4 cup pine nuts, lightly toasted
finely grated zest of 1 lemon
10-12 pitted black olives, chopped

LINE a baking tray with baking parchment. Using a very sharp knife cut a thin slash on an angle on the top of each piece of salmon. Combine parsley, pine nuts, zest and olives and stuff about 1 tbsp mixture into each slash. Cover and chill until ready to cook.

HEAT oven to 220°C / 425°F. Season fish with salt and pepper and squeeze over lemon juice. Bake 6-8 minutes or until just cooked through.

SERVE salmon with a spoonful of Easy Lime Hollandaise and Flash-Roasted Cherry Tomatoes – see side panel. Accompany with Thyme Roasted Baby Potatoes (page 64) and green beans (page 91).

◇ PESTO ROASTED SALMON: For a simpler "on the run" treatment for any oily fish, slather the slashed fillets with pesto, tapenade or salsa verde before roasting.

MARINADES TO ADD FLAVOUR AND TENDERNESS

Marinades are so simple to prepare, yet the qualities they impart – flavour, tenderness and a richly burnished glaze – can transform a simple protein. Allow up to an hour for small cuts and 24-48 hours for whole roasts.

TERIYAKI GLAZED SALMON
In a small pot heat together ¼ cup soy sauce, 2 tbsp sake, 10-12 thin slices fresh ginger, 2 tbsp sugar, the juice of ½ lemon and a little black pepper. Boil until lightly thickened. Cool. Pour mixture over 6 fillets or steaks of salmon. Marinate 1-4 hours in the fridge, turning once or twice.

TERIYAKI GLAZED CHICKEN
Marinate 6 chicken breasts in above teriyaki marinade for 15-60 minutes.

BALSAMIC CHICKEN BREASTS
A delicious marinade for chicken or duck breasts, or beef. Combine 6 boneless chicken breasts with ¼ cup balsamic vinegar and 3 tbsp maple syrup or brown sugar. Leave to marinate in the fridge for at least an hour, or up to 24 hours.

THAI MARINADE FOR BEEF, PORK OR CHICKEN
Makes enough for 1kg / 2 lb meat. Combine 2 tbsp sweet Thai chilli sauce, 3 tbsp soy sauce, 2 tbsp fish sauce, 3 cloves crushed garlic, 1 tbsp grated fresh ginger, the finely grated zest of 1 lime and 2 tbsp olive oil. Season with black pepper. Chill at least 1 hour or up to 24 hours for a whole beef fillet. Drain meat from marinade before cooking.

SPICY VIETNAMESE MARINADE FOR SEAFOOD, BEEF OR CHICKEN
Makes enough for 1kg / 2 lb meat. Heat 2 tbsp vegetable oil in a frypan and sizzle 1 tsp shrimp paste, stirring to break it up. Remove from heat and add 2 tbsp minced fresh ginger, 1 tbsp minced lemon grass, 2 tbsp fish sauce, 3 tbsp brown sugar, finely grated zest of 1 lime or lemon, 8-10 torn mint leaves and 2 minced chillies. Marinade will keep in the fridge up to 2 weeks.

To grill marinated fish steaks:
Place salmon or other fish, skin side down, on a heavy baking sheet. Heat grill. Brush salmon with marinade and grill on the top shelf of the oven for 5-6 minutes, brushing with extra glaze after 4 minutes, until surface is glazy and fish is just cooked through.

To bake marinated chicken breasts:
Bake at 200°C / 400°F for about 20 minutes or until golden and cooked through, brushing with extra marinade or glaze in the last 5 minutes of cooking.

To roast beef: see page 55
To panfry steaks: see page 107

LEFT: Teriyaki Glazed Salmon with rice and stirfried snow peas.

ROASTED VEGETABLES WITH BASIL OIL AND POLENTA WEDGES

FETA AND ROSEMARY POLENTA WEDGES

6 cups water
1 tsp salt and freshly ground pepper
2 cups instant polenta
1 tbsp butter
3/4 cup crumbled feta
1/2 tsp ground nutmeg
1 tsp finely chopped fresh rosemary

Bring water, salt and pepper to the boil in a saucepan. Add polenta in a thin stream as you stir. Cover and cook 3 minutes. Stir in feta, nutmeg and rosemary until evenly combined.

Spread cooked mixture in a shallow, oiled dish to form a 3cm / 1 inch thick slab. Chill until firm. At serving time, cut into wedges and grill or pan fry.

SERVES: 4 PREP TIME: 10-15 minutes COOK TIME: 1 hour 20 minutes
MAKE AHEAD: polenta must be prepared in advance; vegetables can be cooked ahead and briefly reheated to warm through; basil oil can be made up to 5 days ahead and stored in the fridge, or can be frozen

Make this flavoursome platter with whatever vegetables are in season. It makes a very satisfying stand-alone vegetarian meal but is also good served as an accompaniment to roast lamb or beef. Here I have served the vegetables with basil oil. You could also use pesto or Roast Garlic Aioli (page 102).

2 red onions, peeled and cut into 6-8 wedges
4-6 tomatoes, halved
extra virgin olive oil to drizzle
salt and freshly ground black pepper
4-6 flat mushrooms
1 tbsp Basil Oil (page 30) or pesto thinned with a little olive oil
4 roasted red capsicums (bell peppers), peeled and quartered
2 zucchini, cut in paper-thin slices lengthways with a potato peeler
TO SERVE: Feta and Rosemary Polenta Wedges – see side panel
        4 tbsp Basil Oil (page 30)

HEAT oven to 160°C / 325°F. Line a roasting dish with baking parchment. Spread onions and tomatoes, cut-side up, in dish. Drizzle with a little olive oil, turn to coat and season with salt and pepper. Roast 1 hour.

BRUSH mushrooms with basil oil or thinned pesto and add to roasting dish. Roast a further 20 minutes.

WHILE mushrooms are cooking, cut polenta into wedges or triangles. Brush polenta and zucchini with a little olive oil. Heat a grill plate or frypan over medium heat and brown polenta and zucchini on both sides. Add capsicums to grill plate in last few minutes of cooking just to warm through.

TO ASSEMBLE: put 2 pieces of polenta on each plate. Top with vegetables and drizzle with basil oil.

COOK AHEAD

If you are terrified at the prospect of feeding other people, or simply wish to spend as little time as possible in the kitchen once your guests arrive, then this chapter is for you. Food of the "make now, heat and serve later" variety has to be the least stressful way to get a hot meal on the table.

These are the dishes that need to sit for a day or two in the fridge to allow flavours to round out before being reheated and served. It's not so much that they take a lot of effort in preparation, but they do take time. The tough muscular cuts that offer the richest of flavours require long and slow cooking in order to achieve melting tenderness and to release their full taste.

Hearty dishes of bones, slow-cooked meats and gentle, tender pies are our cues for comfort, especially as the weather cools. This is food to line the belly and warm the heart – perfect for a winter Sunday dinner or round-the-fire feast.

It always surprises me how much these homely dishes are appreciated over and above any sophisticated sliver of salmon. In the busy lives we inhabit such undemanding comfort fare soothes and calms the spirit.

Enjoy the cooking process when the pressure is off the weekend before. Also, you can make more than you need and freeze it for another occasion. When it comes to serving these meals it's just a matter of reheating meat and starches and dressing salads.

These are substantial dishes and need little pre-empting. At most serve a light salad to start or simply offer a platter of nibbles with a drink before heading to the table.

LEFT: Chicken and Mushroom Pie (recipe page 92)

BRAISED OXTAILS WITH RED CHILLI BEANS

SERVES: 8 PREP TIME: 20 minutes + soaking of beans
COOK TIME: 4 hours MAKE AHEAD: this dish needs to be made 1-2 days ahead, cooled and the fat removed before reheating

My neighbourhood abounds with laughing kids, great cooks and prolific gardens. Some great friendships have developed over casual neighbourly lunches and dinners. I first enjoyed this dish in such a fashion at the home of good cook Janice Sommerville. It's satisfying comfort food that has everyone sucking bones and licking fingers.

$2^1/2$kg / 5-6 lb oxtails (18-24 pieces), trimmed
salt and freshly ground black pepper
2 tbsp flavourless oil eg grapeseed
2 large onions, finely chopped
1 tbsp crushed garlic
1 tbsp grated root ginger
$3/4$ cup tomato ketchup
$1/3$ cup firmly packed light brown sugar
3 tbsp Dijon mustard
$2/3$ cup cider vinegar or rice vinegar
1 tbsp worcestershire sauce
$1/2$ tsp cayenne pepper or more to taste
3 x 400g / 14 oz cans Italian tomatoes in juice, chopped
$2^1/2$ cups dried red kidney beans, soaked (see panel at left)
GARNISH: chopped parsley

QUICK SOAKING BEANS

Dried beans need to be soaked overnight in enough cold water to cover them by 4.5 cm / $1^1/2$ inches. They can also be quick-soaked on the day.
Fast-soak **beans** by covering them with 4 times the amount of water in a big pot. Bring to the boil, boil 10 minutes then stand 40 minutes. Drain off all the soaking water, cover beans with fresh water and boil hard 5-10 minutes. Reduce heat to a low simmer and continue cooking until beans are tender. Don't add **salt** – it prevents the beans from softening, as do highly acidic ingredients such as tomatoes and citrus juice. Boil beans uncovered – most varieties take about $1-1^1/2$ hours to fully cook. Old beans or hard water will increase the cooking time. Adding a piece of seaweed such as **kombu** to the pot seems to reduce their flatulent effects. Always fully cook beans as undercooked beans are indigestible.

BOIL soaked beans in plenty of fresh water for 30 minutes. Remove from heat and drain off all but 2 cups of liquid. While beans boil, heat oven to 220°C / 425°F. Season oxtails with salt and pepper and spread out in a large roasting dish. Roast about 40 minutes or until oxtails start to brown. Transfer to a large casserole or baking dish, discarding fat.

WHILE oxtails roast, heat oil in a large, heavy pot and cook onions over a moderately low heat, stirring often, until softened. Stir in the beans and the reserved 2 cups of their cooking liquid along with all the remaining ingredients except parsley. Simmer 5 minutes. Transfer to casserole dish with oxtails. Lower oven temperature to 160°C / 325°F. Cover casserole and bake $2^1/2$ hours.

COOL, chill overnight or longer, then remove any fat that sits on top. To reheat, bring back to room temperature then cook 1 hour at 160°C / 325°F.

RIGHT: Braised Oxtails with Red Chilli Beans on Soft Polenta with broccoflower.

know how

THE PLEASURES OF POACHED CHICKEN

Cooling chicken in the liquid it has cooked in is a guaranteed means to a wonderfully moist, tender result that is great for salads or to reheat with an infinite variety of sauces. Vary the flavourings for the broth as preferred – use bay leaves, thyme and peppercorns for a European-style poached chicken, or ginger and spring onions for a more Asian flavour.

ASIAN POACHED CHICKEN BREASTS

PREP TIME: 5 minutes COOK TIME: 8-10 minutes plus cooling
MAKE AHEAD: chicken can be poached up to 2 days ahead and kept chilled

	6 boneless, skinless single chicken breasts
ASIAN	8 slices fresh ginger (cut with a potato peeler)
POACHING	2 spring (green) onions
BROTH	1/2 tsp sesame oil
	1 tsp salt
	several grinds pepper
	4 cups cold water or more as needed to cover
	OPTIONAL: 3-4 whole star anise

PLACE everything in a pot that ideally fits the chicken in a snug, single layer, ensuring there is enough water to fully submerge the chicken. Cover and bring just to the boil. As soon as the liquid comes to the boil take pot off the heat and leave to cool without removing the lid (about 1 1/2 hours). Take chicken out of broth, cover and chill if not using at once. Strain stock and reserve for later use.

◇ FRENCH POACHED CHICKEN BREASTS: Substitute a small handful fresh thyme, 1/2 lemon, 2 bay leaves and 1 small onion for the ginger, spring onions and star anise above.

◇ WHOLE POACHED CHICKEN: Very gently simmer a whole 1.5kg / 3lb chicken for exactly 25 minutes, using enough liquid to fully cover the whole bird by about 3cm / 1 inch. Again, leave to cool in the cooking liquid without removing the lid. Chicken flesh will be pink around the thigh bone but the flesh will be cooked.

VIETNAMESE DRESSING

In a sealed jar shake together 2 tbsp lime juice, 1 tsp fish sauce, 1 tsp brown sugar, 1 tbsp sweet Thai chilli sauce, 1 shredded kaffir lime leaf (or finely grated zest of 1 lime) and a little ground black pepper. Dressing will keep chilled for about a week. Makes 1/4 cup.

ORANGE DRESSING

In a sealed jar shake together the finely grated zest and juice of 1 orange, 2 tbsp flavourless oil such as grapeseed, 2 tsp sherry or rice wine vinegar, 1/2 tsp each salt and sugar, and several grinds of pepper. Dressing will keep chilled for several days. Makes 1/4 cup.

CHICKEN, GRAPES AND WALNUTS

◇ 4 French poached chicken breasts
◇ 1 recipe Orange Dressing (see opposite page) ◇ 500g / 1 lb seedless grapes, halved ◇ 2-3 stems celery, sliced thinly on an angle ◇ ½ cup fresh walnut pieces ◇ 2 tbsp fresh tarragon or chervil leaves

Slice or shred chicken and mix with dressing. When ready to serve mix through grapes, celery, walnuts and herbs. Extend with baby spinach or rocket (arugula) leaves and/or slices of avocado if desired. Although it's very 1970s, a dollop of sour cream and a spoonful of cranberry jelly on top is fabulous.

ASIAN CHICKEN SALAD

Have the chicken poached, the vegetables prepared and dressing made ready for a simple, last minute assembly.

◇ 4 Asian poached chicken breasts
◇ 1 recipe Vietnamese Dressing (see opposite page) ◇ 3 stalks celery, angle sliced ◇ 2 red capsicums (bell peppers), seeded and thinly sliced ◇ 2 spring (green) onions, angle sliced ◇ 2 tablespoons toasted sesame seeds ◇ torn leaves from 2 large sprigs coriander or mint

Slice chicken and mix with dressing. Combine with other ingredients. Serves 6. If you like mix through 250g / 8oz crispy noodles or soft cooked noodles just before serving.

SPICY CHICKEN TAGINE

SERVES: **6 PREP TIME:** 30 minutes plus 45 minutes marinating/soaking
COOK TIME: 40 minutes or 30-35 minutes for chicken pieces
MAKE AHEAD: marinate chicken up to 12 hours ahead

Poussins are baby chickens. They vary in size – the smallest is around 250g / ½ lb, which is ideal for a single portion. Larger poussins can be cut in half. You could also use any bone-in chicken cut in this succulent dish. Reduce the cooking time by 5-10 minutes for half poussins, chicken pieces or breasts.

MOROCCAN MARINADE

¼ cup olive oil

½ cup white wine

2 tsp ground cumin

1 tsp chilli powder

1 tsp salt and freshly ground
   black pepper

1 lemon, juice and finely grated
   zest

Combine all ingredients. Use as a marinade for chicken, duck or pork.

6 whole poussins or chicken supremes, breasts or legs
1 recipe Moroccan Marinade - see side panel
2 cinnamon sticks, broken into pieces
2 tsp crushed garlic
400g / 15oz can tomatoes in juice, chopped
2 cups well-seasoned chicken stock
good pinch saffron threads
12-15 dried apricots or prunes, thinly sliced
OPTIONAL: 2 tsp melted honey to glaze birds
TO SERVE: 2 cups prepared couscous eg Almond and Chickpea
   Couscous – see side panel
GARNISHES: 400g / 15oz tender young green beans
flesh of 2 red and 2 yellow capsicums (bell peppers),
   roasted and sliced in thin strips
¼ cup chopped fresh coriander (cilantro) and/or mint

ALMOND AND CHICKPEA COUSCOUS

1½ cups boiling water

juice and zest of 1 lemon

1 tsp salt

1½ cups couscous

400g / 15oz can chickpeas, rinsed and drained

½ cup toasted almonds, chopped

⅓ cup chopped mint or coriander

Place boiling water, lemon juice, zest and salt in a bowl and mix in couscous. Stir well and leave for 10 minutes. Break up with a fork, rubbing between fingers to remove any lumpy bits. Mix in other ingredients. Serves 6. Reheats well, covered in the oven or microwave.

PLACE chicken in a clean plastic bag with marinade. Place pieces of cinnamon in bird cavities or if using chicken pieces mix through marinade. Seal and chill 12-24 hours.

HEAT oven to 200°C / 400°F. Place drained chicken in a roasting dish in a single layer. Heat marinade with garlic, tomatoes, stock, saffron and apricots or prunes. Pour over chicken and bake 30-40 minutes or until cooked through and golden. Brush melted honey over birds in last 5 minutes of cooking to glaze. While chicken cooks prepare the couscous.

JUST before serving, drop beans into a pot of boiling water and cook 2 minutes. To serve, place couscous on serving plates or one large platter, put beans and capsicums on top with chicken, spoon over any sauce and scatter over coriander or mint. Serve at once.

SPICY ONE-DISH DINING

Make these flavoursome one-dish meals a day or two ahead and savour their exotic, spicy richness. Cook each recipe ahead to the stage where it is marked ◇ and then cool, cover and chill, or freeze.

THAI CHICKEN CURRY

Heat 2 tbsp vegetable oil in a large, heavy pot and fry 1-2 tbsp green curry paste (or to taste), 2 tsp minced fresh ginger and the finely grated zest of 1 lime for about a minute. Add 400ml / 15oz can coconut cream, 1 cup chicken stock, 2 tbsp fish sauce and 2 kaffir lime leaves (optional). Simmer 10 minutes. ◇ When ready to serve, bring sauce back to a simmer and add 1kg boneless, skinless chicken thighs, thinly sliced, 250g green beans and 225g / 8oz can bamboo shoot slices, rinsed and drained or a 225g / 8oz can straw mushrooms, drained. Season with salt and pepper and stir well. Once chicken comes to a simmer, reduce heat, cover pot tightly and leave to cook on lowest possible heat for 5-6 minutes or until the chicken is fully cooked. Adjust seasoning to taste. Serve curry garnished with 1/4 cup chopped coriander. Serves 6. Accompany with rice.

FRAGRANT LAMB TAGINE

Cut 1 1/2 kg / 3lb lean lamb into 5cm / 2 inch cubes. Place in a medium casserole dish or heavy saucepan with 2 tbsp good quality commercial Moroccan spice mix, the finely grated zest of 1 lemon, 6 whole cloves, 6 cardamom pods, 1 cinnamon stick, 1 tsp chilli flakes, 3 cloves crushed garlic, 12-14 dried apricots, chopped, 1 1/2 cups chicken stock and 400g / 15oz can tomatoes in juice, chopped. Season with salt and pepper. Bring to a boil, stir, cover and simmer gently for 1 hour. If using the oven, cover and bake 1 1/2 hours at 160°C / 325°F or until meat is tender. Adjust seasoning to taste. ◇ When ready to serve simmer a further 30 minutes or bake at 160°C / 325°F for 45 minutes to fully heat through. Mix in the juice of 1/2 lemon and 2 tbsp chopped coriander just before serving. Serves 6. Accompany with couscous.

FISH CURRY

In a food processor purée together: 1/2 cup coconut cream, 1/3 cup desiccated coconut, 1/2 cup roasted cashews, 1 tsp brown sugar, 1-2 seeded green chillies, 2 cups coriander leaves, juice and zest of 2-3 limes, 3 cloves garlic, 2 tbsp chopped fresh ginger, 1/2 tsp ground turmeric, 1 tbsp cumin seeds, 1 tsp salt and 2 cups fish stock or chicken stock. Simmer 10 minutes. ◇ When ready to serve bring back to a simmer and add 2 medium potatoes, cut in 3cm dice and 225g / 8oz peeled, seeded pumpkin, cut in 2-3cm pieces. Simmer gently for 20 minutes. Add 500g / 1lb fresh, white, skinless fish fillets, sliced in 3-4 cm chunks. Stir well, cover and cook 5 minutes without stirring until fish is cooked through. Spoon into serving bowls and top with lightly cooked green beans. Serves 4. Accompany with rice.

LEFT: Fish Curry

87

BRAISED LAMB SHANKS WITH GARLIC AND PORT

SERVES: 4-6 PREP TIME: 15 minutes COOK TIME: 3 hours
MAKE AHEAD: shanks can be cooked up to 2 days ahead and kept chilled, or frozen for longer.

There's nothing arduous about cooking these shanks yet the results – a sticky melt-in-the-mouth tenderness and deep, rich flavour – are arrestingly good.

> 2 tbsp flour
> salt and freshly ground black pepper
> 8 lamb shanks
> 3 tbsp oil
> 4 whole heads garlic, halved crosswise
> 2 tbsp tomato paste
> 1 tsp brown sugar
> few drops hot pepper sauce
> 1½ cups (half bottle) full-bodied red wine
> 1 cup port
> 2 sprigs rosemary, stalks removed and leaves chopped
> 2 cups beef or lamb stock

PREHEAT oven to 180°C / 350°F. Place flour in a clean plastic bag with salt and a generous grind of pepper. Add shanks and shake to lightly coat.

HEAT oil in a large, heavy-based pan and brown shanks in batches. Transfer to a large baking dish along with garlic halves.

DISCARD excess fat from pan, add tomato paste and cook a minute or two to let the flavour develop. Add remaining ingredients and bring to a fast simmer. Stir well to lift any pan sediments then pour over meat. Cover and bake for 2 hours (or if serving at once and not reheating, cook for 2½-3 hours or until very tender).

COOL, chill then remove any fat that sits on top. To reheat, bring back to room temperature then cook a further 1 hour at 160°C / 325°F. Serve shanks with a garlic half and sauce. Accompany with Mash (page 90) and Peas and Beans (see side panel).

VARIATION: separate and peel raw garlic cloves and add to the sauce before baking shanks.

PEAS AND BEANS

Use a combination of **peas** and **podded broad beans** or **green soya beans**, allowing about ⅓ cup per serve. Place in a pot and pour over boiling **water** to cover. Drain off all but about 2 tbsp **water**. Add a splash of **extra virgin olive oil** or a knob of **butter**, a shake of **sea salt** and a grinding of **black pepper**. Cover and cook 2-3 minutes or until liquid has evaporated. Add torn mint or basil leaves and serve.

TOSSED GREEN SALAD

Wash and dry salad greens and store in a plastic bag in the fridge. Provided they are dry, they will keep fresh for over a week. When you want a salad, simply take greens out of the bag and toss with just enough **Balsamic Dressing** (page 22) to coat. Add wedges of **avocado**, halved **cherry tomatoes**, thinly sliced **spring (green) onions**, chopped **herbs** or **toasted nuts** as desired and lightly toss. Be sure to dress the salad just before you plan to serve it or it will wilt.

RIGHT: Braised Lamb Shanks with Garlic and Port served on Kumara (Sweet Potato) Mash (page 90) with Peas and Beans (see side panel).

MORE ON THE SIDE

Save time and take the last minute panic out of serving up by making mash or potato grain and reheating, or parboiling root vegetables before roasting.

MASH
Cooked mash can be reheated for 5 minutes in a microwave. Add a little more hot milk if needed.

Peel 7-8 medium-sized potatoes and cut into chunks. Boil in salted water until tender. Drain thoroughly. Use a potato masher or fork to mash with 2-3 tbsp butter and ¼ cup hot milk or cream, mashing until creamy and smooth. (Do not use a food processor.) Season to taste. If not using at once, cover and chill. Serves 6. Flavour mash as desired with: truffle oil, Roasted Garlic (page 97), Basil Oil (page 30) or a flavoured butter (page 48).
◇ KUMARA (SWEET POTATO) MASH: replace half the potatoes with peeled, chopped kumara (sweet potato).
◇ CELERIAC MASH: replace half the potatoes with peeled, chopped celeriac. Good with fish.

GARLICKY POTATO GRATIN
Fresh herbs can be used in place of garlic for this satisfying potato dish.

Thinly slice 1.3kg / about 3lb peeled, floury potatoes. Layer in a large, buttered baking dish, seasoning with salt and pepper between the layers. Crush 3 cloves garlic and mix with 3 cups milk, ½ tsp grated nutmeg and 2 tbsp chopped parsley. Pour over potatoes, adding more milk if needed to almost cover the top layer. Dot with butter, cover and microwave 10 minutes then uncover and bake 45-50 minutes at 200°C / 400°F until golden and tender. If you don't have a microwave, bake about 1¼ hours. Gratin can be cooked ahead of time, cooled and shapes cut out with a round cutter if desired. Reheat in the oven or microwave.

TENDER GREENS

The greatest flavour can be extracted from vegetables when they are cooked to al dente – tender, but with a bite. Follow this method for any green vegetable or medley of vegetables.

Allow about 100g / 3-4oz fresh beans, broccoli and/or asparagus per serve. Trim beans, cut broccoli into florets and snap off and discard tough ends of asparagus. Place vegetables in a saucepan with 2 tbsp extra virgin olive oil or butter and ⅓ cup water. Season. Cover and cook over high heat for 5-6 minutes or until vegetables are just tender but still green and water has evaporated. Serve at once.
◇ WILTED SPINACH: Heat 2 tbsp olive oil in a frypan. Add 500g / 1 lb wet spinach leaves, cover and cook until wilted. Season with salt, pepper and a little nutmeg. Serves 6.

ROAST ROOT VEGETABLES AND PUMPKIN

Allow about 4-5 chunky pieces of vegetable per serve. For root vegetables choose from kumara (sweet potatoes), parsnips, pumpkin, yams and beets.

Peel vegetables and cut into chunks or fat batons. (If using beets leave unpeeled and keep them to one side as their colour will bleed into other vegetables). Drop vegetables into a pot of lightly salted boiling water for 3 minutes. Drain thoroughly. Chill until ready to use. Place in a large roasting dish. Mix through about 2 tbsp olive oil and season with a little rock salt. Spread out in dish to a single layer. Drizzle with 1-2 tbsp maple syrup or honey. Roast at 200°C / 400°F for about 20 minutes then increase temperature to 220°C / 425°F and cook a further 10 minutes to brown and crisp.
◇ ROAST POTATOES: see page 64.

STEAK AND KIDNEY PIE

This is comfort food just like granny used to make. To cook the meat you'll need a large metal basin that will fit inside a larger saucepan. The technique is a great way to cook tougher meat – you can use it for any slow-cooking cut.

Place 1kg / 2 lb **blade or chuck steak**, cut in 4cm / 1½ inch dice, and 6 **lambs' kidneys**, cut into pieces in a metal basin with 3 large **onions**, thinly sliced, 300g / 1¼ cups **mushrooms**, sliced, 2 tbsp **sherry, port or water**, 1 tsp **salt**, several grinds **pepper**, 2 **bay leaves** and 2 tsp chopped **fresh thyme** or 1 tsp **dried thyme**. Cover with foil.
Place basin inside a large saucepan filled with enough water to reach about halfway up the sides. Cover saucepan tightly and cook over medium-low heat for 2 hours. Watch that the pan doesn't boil dry and add more water as necessary.
Twenty minutes before meat is cooked, remove bay leaves and stir in 2 tbsp **cornflour (cornstarch)** mixed with a little water. Add **salt and pepper** to taste. At serving time garnish with ¼ cup chopped **parsley**.
Serve topped with cooked **pastry cut-outs (page 18)** and accompany with **mash (page 90)**. Serves 5-6. Freezes well. This pie can also be cooked in a pressure cooker – it will take 15 minutes.

CHICKEN AND MUSHROOM PIE

SERVES: 6-8 PREP TIME: 15 minutes COOK TIME: 1 hour and 10 minutes
MAKE AHEAD: cook sauce up to 24 hours ahead or freeze

Rich with the flavours of baby onions, red wine, mushrooms and herbs, this dish is just the thing for a cold winter's night around the fire. I prefer to cook the pastry on top of the pie and have it soft and gravied on the underside, probably for nostalgic reasons over any other, as that's how my mother always made her pies. If you prefer, cook the pastry separately, either the same size as the pie or as single-serve pieces.

> 2 tbsp olive oil
> 400g / 14oz button mushrooms, wiped with a damp cloth
> 3 strips bacon, diced
> 8-10 baby onions, peeled and halved
> 8-10 cloves garlic (small head), peeled and halved lengthways
> 400g / 14oz can tomatoes in juice, chopped
> 1½ cups red wine
> 3 cups good chicken stock
> HERBS: 1 tsp finely chopped fresh rosemary, 2 tsp finely chopped fresh
>   thyme, 2 tbsp finely chopped Italian parsley and 2-3 bay leaves
> 1 tsp salt
> freshly ground black pepper to taste
> 3 tbsp cornflour (cornstarch)
> 2 tbsp port or red wine
> 800g / 1½ lb boneless, skinless chicken thighs, quartered
> 400g / 14oz puff pastry
> 1 egg, beaten or a little milk to glaze

HEAT oil in a large, heavy pan. Add mushrooms and bacon. Brown well, then remove and set aside. Add onions and garlic to pan and cook gently 8-10 minutes or until onion is softened and starting to brown.

ADD tomatoes and their juice, wine, stock, herbs, seasonings and browned mushrooms and bacon. Simmer gently 20 minutes. Combine cornflour and port or wine and mix into sauce, stirring over heat until lightly thickened. Adjust seasonings to taste. Cool. Sauce can be prepared ahead of time to this point, cooled and chilled or frozen.

HEAT oven to 200°C / 400°F. Place raw chicken in a large, shallow baking or pie dish. Pour over cooled sauce and mix until evenly combined. Roll out pastry to cover top of dish. Cut a 3cm / 1 inch strip of pastry and run it around the edge to form a double layered rim. Crimp this with your thumbs or a fork. If desired garnish top with pastry leaf cut-outs. Brush with egg or milk to glaze and cut a few steam vent holes. Bake 40-45 minutes or until pastry is golden and crispy.

FISH AND SCALLOP PIE WITH CREAMY LEMON SAUCE AND CAPER CRUMB

SERVES: 6 PREP TIME: 15 minutes COOK TIME: 30-35 minutes
MAKE AHEAD: pie can be assembled ready to cook up to 12 hours ahead

This wonderfully soothing pie combines lemony sauce, fresh seafood and crisp crumbs. I've opted for a rather extravagant version here that includes scallops but you can just use all fish and if necessary extend the pie with some halved hard-boiled eggs. It's a great dish to have in the refrigerator ready to bake at serving time and just the sort of thing to serve to anyone needing some TLC comfort fare.

1/2 tsp grated or ground nutmeg
80ml / 1/3 cup lemon juice (or more to taste)
4 cups well-seasoned Gourmet White Sauce - see side panel
800g-1kg / 11/2–2 lb fresh, thick boneless fish fillets,
    cut in 3-4cm / 1–2 inch dice
OPTIONAL: 100g-150g / 31/2-5oz scallops or other seafood

CAPER
CRUMB

4 toast slices white bread
1/4 cup melted butter, or oil
2 tbsp chopped capers
finely grated zest of 1 lemon
salt and freshly ground black pepper

MIX nutmeg and lemon juice into white sauce – it should be quite runny and very lemony in flavour.

HEAT oven to 200°C / 400°F. Mix raw seafood into sauce and pour mixture into a large pie dish. (If preparing ahead to this stage, allow sauce to cool before combining with the fish, pour into pie dish, cover and chill.)

CAPER CRUMB: In a food processor, blitz together bread and butter or oil, capers and zest until they form a fine crumb. Season with salt and pepper and sprinkle over pie.

BAKE 30-35 minutes or until sauce bubbles around edges and crumbs turn golden. (If preparing ahead, assemble pie ready to bake and chill. It will take about 40 minutes to cook from the fridge.)

LEFT: Fish and Scallop Pie with green beans
and Garlicky Potato Gratin (page 90).

GOURMET WHITE SAUCE

100g / 31/2oz butter
6 tbsp flour
4 cups milk
1 tsp salt
1/4 tsp white pepper
1/4 tsp ground nutmeg
250g / 1/2 lb light sour cream

Melt butter in a heavy pan. Add flour and stir over heat for a couple of minutes. Gradually add milk, stirring constantly, and cook until sauce is smooth and thickened. Simmer 2-3 minutes. Season well with salt, pepper and nutmeg and mix in sour cream. If not using at once, cool, cover and chill up to 24 hours.

FRAGRANT RICE

2 cups jasmine rice
3 cups water
1 tsp salt
2 stalks lemongrass or 2 kaffir lime
    leaves, or finely grated zest of
    1 lime

Place rice in a pot with water, salt and lemongrass. Bring to a simmer, stir well then cover tightly and cook over lowest heat 12-15 minutes. Take off heat and stand up to 15 minutes. Fluff with a fork and remove flavourings before serving. Serves 6.

menu 8

USEFUL STARTING POINTS

Keep these items in your fridge for last-minute meals. They make great beginnings for impromptu dining and offer a useful flavour boost.

ROASTED TOMATO SAUCE
A wonderful one-step sauce to store in the fridge or freeze. Use for pasta or any time you want a rich tomato flavour.

Heat oven to 160°C / 325°F. Place 1.5kg / 3 lb tomatoes, cored and quartered, and 2 large onions, peeled and sliced in thin wedges, in a big mixing bowl. Purée together 140g-150g / 10 tbsp tomato paste, 4-5 cloves garlic, peeled, ½ cup olive oil, 1 tbsp sugar, 1 tbsp white wine vinegar, 1 tsp salt and several grinds black pepper until smooth. Mix evenly through tomatoes and onions. Spread mixture in a single layer in a roasting dish lined with baking parchment. Bake about 1½ hours or until slightly browned. Purée sauce until smooth. Store in a clean container in the fridge or freezer.

ROASTED STUFFED CAPSICUMS (BELL PEPPERS)
Make these in bulk and store them in the fridge.

Heat oven to 160°C / 325°F. Place 3 large red capsicums (bell peppers), halved, seeded and pith removed, cut side up on a baking tray. Combine 1 large clove garlic, finely crushed, 2-3 large anchovies, chopped, 1 tbsp salted capers, soaked, drained and chopped, ½ tsp minced chilli or dried chilli flakes (optional) and 6-8 tsp extra virgin olive oil. Divide over the top of peppers. Bake 40-45 minutes or until capsicums are soft and aromatic but not browned. Cool. They will keep in the fridge for about a week. ◇ WHOLE ROASTED CAPSICUMS: Place whole capsicums in a baking tray. Bake at 220°C / 400°F for about 20 minutes until skins start to blister and brown. Cool and remove skins, seeds and pith. Chill for a few days or freeze.

BALSAMIC CARAMEL ONIONS

Peel 4 red onions, halve then cut into thin wedges. Place in heavy pan with 2 tbsp olive oil, 2 tbsp brown sugar, 1 tbsp balsamic vinegar, ½ cup water, ½ tsp finely chopped rosemary leaves, ½ tsp salt and several grinds black pepper. Cover and cook gently for 10 minutes. Remove lid, stir and cook a further 5-8 minutes, gently stirring now and then. Cook until water has evaporated. These will keep in the fridge for a couple of weeks. Makes about 2 cups.

◇ ROASTED GARLIC Cut 3 whole heads of unpeeled garlic in half horizontally. Place in a baking dish and pour over 1 cup olive oil. Cover and bake at 160°C / 325°F for 30 minutes. Pop garlic out of skins to use. Keeps in the fridge for several weeks. Use the oil in dressings or where you want a sweet garlic flavour.

SWEET AND SOUR MUSTARD SEED SAUCE

This incredibly versatile sauce makes an ideal partner to most meats. It keeps for at least a week in the fridge and can also be frozen. If capsicums (bell peppers) are out of season you can substitute diced red onion.

Cut up 1 red capsicum (bell pepper), seeds and pith removed, into 3cm / 1 inch pieces. Heat 1 tbsp olive oil in a heavy pan and cook capsicum 1-2 minutes or until softened. Add ½ cup sugar, 1 cup red wine, ⅓ cup red wine vinegar, 2 tsp mustard seeds and 1 tbsp dried currants and bring to a fast boil. Simmer about 15 minutes or until sauce is reduced by about a third. Cool, cover and chill if not using at once.

LAST MINUTE

Some cooks operate on the theory that the more time and effort they lavish on a dish the better it will be. I reserve this strategy for rare occasions when I have all day to potter in the kitchen. The rest of the time I go for "high performance" food – ingredients that offer serious appetite appeal but require minimal effort in the kitchen.

A can of beluga caviar is the speediest means to achieve the effect of angels dancing on tongues but if you didn't score at the pokies, adjust your sights more modestly to a perfectly cooked steak, tender lamb cutlet or freshest fillet of fish. The sow's ear, silk purse rule applies. Start off with the best quality ingredients and your job in the kitchen will be easy.

Assemble a starter, if you so choose to serve one – a platter of freshest oysters or wedges of sweet, ripe melon and finely sliced prosciutto; sliced cherry tomatoes, mozzarella and basil with a drizzle of the very best olive oil, a perfect avocado with balsamic dressing, smoked salmon and bread. Or you can simply pick up some nibbly bits from the local deli.

Roast a tender rack of lamb and serve with a fresh chilli mint salsa (page 60), pop a chicken breast in a tangy marinade for half an hour then throw it in the oven to roast (page 75), grill a piece of tender salmon with a coating of sweet chilli sauce and a squeeze of lime juice (page 72), or slather some scallops with flavoured butter (page 48), whack them under the grill for a couple of minutes and toss through freshly cooked slithery noodles. More ideas along these lines can be found in the roasting chapter which starts on page 50.

Finish off with grilled fruit or a fresh fruit salad, ice cream and a yummy sauce, or grab a gourmet dessert from the cake shop on the way home.

On these next few pages you'll find some simple stovetop ideas for impromptu guests.

LEFT: Pronto Pasta with Pine Nuts and Tomatoes (recipe page 100)

PUTTANESCA

Heat ¼ cup **extra virgin olive oil** in a large, deep frypan. Gently fry 4 cloves minced **garlic** and 6 **anchovies** for 3-4 minutes, until anchovies are pasty and garlic is starting to colour. Mix in 1 cup **Roasted Tomato Sauce** (page 96) or commercial tomato pasta sauce. Simmer 5 minutes then add 1 tbsp **capers**, 1 tbsp **pitted and chopped tasty black olives**, and ½-1 tsp **chilli flakes**. Simmer another 5 minutes, stirring occasionally. Adjust seasoning to taste. Serve with spaghetti. Serves 4.

BOLOGNAISE

Great with spaghetti or in lasagne.

Brown about 450g / 1 lb **steak mince** in a large heavy pan, breaking up finely. Add 2 tbsp **tomato paste**, 2 cups **Roasted Tomato Sauce** (page 96) or commercial **tomato pasta sauce**, 1 cup **red wine**, 100g / 4oz **chicken liver pâté** (optional), 2 tbsp **Basil Oil** (page 30) or **pesto**, 2 tsp **dried oregano** and 2 tsp **red wine vinegar**. Season with **salt** and **pepper**. Simmer gently for half an hour, stirring to prevent catching. Serve with spaghetti. Serves 4.

menu 9

100

PASTA WITH SALMON, CAPERS AND ROCKET

SERVES: 4 PREP TIME: 5 minutes COOK TIME: 10 minutes
MAKE AHEAD: This is a last minute assembly

> 400-500g / about 1 lb fettuccini or pappardelle noodles
> 2 tbsp extra virgin olive oil
> 3 tbsp capers
> 200g / 7oz baby rocket (arugula) leaves, washed
> salt and freshly ground black pepper
> 450g / about 1 lb hot smoked salmon, bones removed and flesh coarsely
>   flaked
> finely grated zest of 1 lemon
> 2-3 tbsp lemon juice

COOK pasta in plenty of boiling, salted water according to packet instructions. While pasta cooks, heat oil and fry capers until crunchy. Transfer to a plate. Add rocket to pan, season with salt and pepper and cook just until wilted.

DRAIN pasta and toss with fried capers, salmon, lemon zest and juice. Season with salt and pepper. Divide between serving plates and top with a little rocket.

PRONTO PASTA WITH PINE NUTS AND TOMATOES

SERVES: 4 PREP TIME: 10 minutes COOK TIME: 10-12 minutes for pasta
MAKE AHEAD: This is a last minute assembly

> 400-500g / about 1 lb dried pasta, eg buccatini
> ¼ cup extra virgin olive oil
> 2 zucchini, thinly sliced
> ½ cup pine nuts, toasted
> 400g / 14oz red and yellow cherry tomatoes, halved
> ¼ cup Basil Oil (page 30) or pesto thinned with olive oil
> 100g / 4oz feta cheese, crumbled
> 2 tbsp lemon juice
> salt and freshly ground black pepper

COOK pasta in plenty of boiling, salted water according to packet instructions. While pasta cooks, heat oil and fry zucchini over high heat for a couple of minutes until they change colour. Drain pasta. Toss with zucchini and all other ingredients. Season to taste. Serve at once.

know how

DRIED BREADCRUMBS

Good quality, freshly dried and slightly chunky white breadcrumbs make all the difference to a crumb crust. Dry slices of **stale white bread** in a 120°C / 250°F oven for about an hour or until completely crisp but not brown. Beat in a closed plastic bag or process to a rough crumb. Store in an airtight container or freeze.

GREMOLATA CRUMB

Try these for a tasty change from a plain breadcrumb crust. Mix 1 cup dried **chunky white breadcrumbs** with the finely grated zest of 1 **lemon**, 2 tsp chopped **capers** and 1 tbsp finely **chopped fresh parsley** or mint.

ROAST GARLIC AIOLI

A wonderful partner for salads and meat dishes. Mix 2 **egg yolks**, 3 tbsp **lemon juice**, 1/2 tsp **salt** and a few grinds of **black pepper** in a blender or food processor until smooth. With motor running slowly add 1 cup **flavourless oil, eg grapeseed**, and 1/2 cup **extra virgin olive oil**. Process until thick. Blend in the flesh from 1 head **roasted garlic** (page 97). Adjust seasonings to taste. Chill. Makes about 2 cups. Keeps up to 2 weeks.

MAKING A CRUST

Whether for schnitzel, lamb cutlets, fish or chicken, the method for making a crumb crust is the same. Use lightly beaten egg or egg white to attach the crumb and be sure to chill the crumbed meat before cooking.

POLENTA AND PARMESAN-CRUSTED FISH

SERVES: 4 PREP TIME: 10 minutes plus 30 minutes chilling COOK TIME: 5-8 minutes
MAKE AHEAD: fish can be crumbed up to 8 hours ahead and kept chilled

	4 fillets freshest white fish
	1 egg white, beaten until frothy
POLENTA	1/4 cup freshly grated parmesan
AND	1/3 cup polenta or coarse cornmeal
PARMESAN	1/2 tsp salt
CRUST	freshly ground black pepper
	2 tbsp olive oil or clarified butter
	TO SERVE: Sicilian Parsley Salad – see opposite page

DIP fish fillets into egg white to lightly coat all over then coat with combined parmesan, polenta, salt and pepper. Place on a plate lined with plastic wrap. Cover and chill at least 30 minutes or up to 8 hours before cooking.

HEAT oil or butter in a large, heavy frypan and cook fish over medium heat about 2 minutes each side or until golden and crunchy and cooked through. Drain on paper towels. If fillets are very thick and meaty, transfer browned fillets to a hot oven for 2 minutes to complete cooking. Serve with Sicilian Parsley Salad (pictured right).

GREMOLATA LAMB CUTLETS
◇ 16 lamb cutlets ◇ ¼ cup flour
◇ salt and pepper ◇ 2 eggs, lightly
beaten ◇ gremolata breadcrumbs
(see side panel) ◇ oil for frying

Coat cutlets with seasoned flour. Shake
off excess. Dip in eggs then in gremolata
breadcrumbs to cover liberally on both
sides. Chill until ready to cook. Heat
½cm oil in a heavy pan and fry cutlets
over medium-high heat about 2 minutes
each side or until golden and crisp. Add
more oil to the pan as needed to ensure
the cutlets lightly fry. Drain on paper
towels. Serve with Roast Garlic Aioli
(see opposite page) and greens. Serves 4.

SICILIAN PARSLEY SALAD
An excellent partner to roasted and
grilled seafood and meats, or mixed
through prepared couscous. Make salad
ahead of time without the lemon juice
and chill in a sealed container. Dress
with lemon juice at serving time. For a
simple starter add 6-8 chopped radishes
to salad and accompany with crostini
spread with goats' cheese.

◇ 1 packed cup Italian parsley leaves, no
stems ◇ 2 tbsp tiny capers (nonpareilles)
◇ 8-10 tasty black olives, pitted and
roughly chopped ◇ ½ medium red onion,
halved and cut into very thin wedges,
◇ 2 tbsp pine nuts, toasted

Toss everything together. At serving
time dress with the juice of ½ lemon.
Makes about 1½ cups.

PENANG-STYLE SEAFOOD LAKSA

SERVES: 4 PREP TIME: 5 minutes COOK TIME: 10 minutes
MAKE AHEAD: sauce can be made (ready to cook seafood) up to a day ahead and chilled or frozen

Southeast Asian food achieves complex and satisfying flavours through the use of aromatics such as garlic, ginger, chilli and – most importantly – fermented fish products like fish sauce and/or dried shrimp. Though they smell stinky in the jar, these fish products render a delicious and odourless richness to any sauce. Make up the sauce for this terrific laksa ahead of time.

LAKSA SAUCE

Add whatever fish, chicken or vegetables you like to this fabulous sauce base. Sauce will keep for a couple of days in the fridge. Makes enough for 4 serves.

2 tbsp flavourless vegetable oil
1 tsp green curry paste,
   or more to taste
2 tsp minced fresh ginger
1 tsp ground turmeric
optional: 1 tbsp finely chopped
   dried shrimp
1 tbsp fish sauce
1 tsp brown sugar
2 fresh kaffir lime leaves,
   or finely grated zest 1 lime
1 red chilli, seeded and flesh
   finely chopped
400ml / 14oz can coconut cream
2 cups fish or chicken stock
salt and freshly ground black
   pepper

Heat oil and cook curry paste, ginger, turmeric and dried shrimp for a few seconds.
Add all the other ingredients and simmer 5 minutes. Season well with salt and pepper. Cool, cover and chill for up to 2 days if not using at once, or freeze.

1 recipe Laksa Sauce – see side panel
400-500g / about 1 lb freshest boneless white fleshed fish,
   diced in 3-4cm / 1-2 inch chunks
12 large shrimp or prawn tails
100g-150g / 4-5oz scallops or 150g / 5oz squid tubes, thinly sliced
300g / 11oz udon noodles or other fresh soft noodles

GARNISH 3 tbsp chopped coriander (cilantro) or mint
1 cup bean sprouts
2 x 4cm / 1½ inch pieces cucumber, cut lengthways into matchsticks

PLACE laksa sauce in a large pot and bring to a simmer. Add seafood and simmer gently for 5 minutes.

WHILE sauce simmers, place noodles in a bowl and cover with boiling water to soften and heat through. If dried, cook as per packet directions, taking care not to overcook.

DRAIN noodles thoroughly and add to pot. Stir gently to combine and bring back to a simmer. Divide laksa between heated serving bowls and spoon over extra liquids. Combine garnish ingredients and pile on top.

COOK'S NOTE: If using squid or scallops add these in the last minute of cooking the fish.

◇ CHICKEN LAKSA: Use diced chicken in place of seafood, and simmer until fully cooked.

◇ VEGETARIAN LAKSA: Use 500g chopped root vegetables eg: potato, kumara (sweet potato) and pumpkin and 200g green beans in place of seafood. Cook until vegetables are tender.

STEAK & SAUCES

It's the simplest meal yet one that always wins applause from meat lovers. Whether it's beef, venison, pork or lamb, to ensure tenderness you'll need either scotch fillet (rib-eye), porterhouse or T-bone, sirloin or fillet.

COOKING THE PERFECT STEAK

Take 4-6 tender beef or venison steaks, cut about 5cm-7cm / 2-2½ inches thick, and season well with salt and ground black pepper.

Heat a heavy pan with 1 tbsp butter or olive oil and quickly brown steaks on each side. Remove from pan and cool if not serving at once.

Heat oven to 200°C / 400°F, place steaks in a baking pan and cook 8-10 minutes to finish (see page 55 for degrees of doneness). Cover and rest 5 minutes. Serves 4-6. (If you are on the run, cut steaks thinner – 3cm / 1½ inches – and cook in hot pan for 2 minutes each side for a juicy pink result.)

Use the frypan you have browned your steak in for the sauce – the pan brownings will add lots of flavour.

ROASTED MUSHROOM SAUCE

Panfry 300g / 11oz fresh button mushrooms in 2 tbsp olive oil with 1 clove crushed garlic until lightly browned. Add 1-2 tbsp brandy, 2 cups good beef stock and 5-6 dried mushrooms such as porcini (optional) that have been soaked for 20 minutes in ¼ cup red wine. Boil hard for about 5 minutes or until sauce is reduced by about a third. Season to taste with salt and pepper. Mix 2 tsp cornflour (cornstarch) with a little water and mix into sauce, stirring over heat until lightly thickened. (Add a little cream if you like). Adjust seasonings to taste. Makes 2 cups, serves 6.

CREAMY GORGONZOLA SAUCE

Heat 1 cup cream with 100g crumbled gorgonzola or other blue cheese, swirling over heat until cheese is melted. Sauce thickens on cooling. It will keep several days in the fridge. Warm to reheat. Makes 1½ cups.

BRANDY PEPPERCORN SAUCE

Heat 1 tbsp butter and gently cook 1 finely diced shallot for 5 minutes. Add 1 tbsp brandy and ignite. When flames subside add 1 cup chicken stock, ½ cup cream and 1 tsp green peppercorns. Boil hard for 5 minutes or until sauce will coat the back of a spoon. (If you boil the sauce too far it will separate, in which case mix in a little more cream.) Season to taste with salt and pepper. Makes ¾ cup.

BALSAMIC ONION SAUCE

Simmer together ½ recipe balsamic caramelised onions (page 97), 2 cups beef stock, and ¼ cup port. Thicken with 1 tsp cornflour (cornstarch) mixed with a little water. Season to taste. Makes 3 cups.

LEFT: Venison steak with Roasted Mushroom Sauce, Wilted Spinach (page 91), and Potato and Goats' Cheese Rosti (page 65).

CREAMY RISOTTO AND SEVERAL STUNNING VARIATIONS

MUSHROOM RISOTTO

Soak 5-6 slices dried mushrooms such as porcini (ceps) for at least 15 minutes in ¼ cup white wine. Heat 3 tbsp butter in a pan and gently cook 500g / ½ lb mixed fresh mushrooms, thinly sliced, until lightly browned. Add soaked dried mushrooms and their liquid and cook until all the liquid has evaporated. Season to taste before adding to risotto.

DUCK AND MUSHROOM RISOTTO

If you get hit by a moment of extravagance, buy a roasted duck from an Asian grocer and shred the meat into the risotto at the same time as you add the mushrooms. (Crisp the skin and toss into a salad to serve with the risotto.)

BLUE CHEESE RISOTTO

Gently melt together 150g / 5oz blue cheese and 1 cup cream. Stir this into risotto 5 minutes before it has finished cooking in place of the mushrooms. Garnish with fried sage leaves.

BLUE CHEESE AND MUSHROOM RISOTTO

Add both cooked mushroom mix and blue cheese sauce to risotto.

SERVES: 4-5 PREP TIME: 10 minutes plus soaking COOK TIME: 25 minutes
MAKE AHEAD: best made at the last minute

And now for perhaps the most demanding dish in this entire book. Risotto requires your undivided attention. Five minutes too long cooking and you end up with gloop; not enough stock and the risotto gets brittle and dry. Sounds scary, but in fact it's not so much a tricky technique as a matter of timing. You need to be in the kitchen keeping an eye on it and once it's ready you need to eat it straight away. Get these things sorted and risotto is one of the utterly soothing, most pleasurable of dishes so I have included it, along with as much information as possible to help you get it right. As to whether to serve this sloppy like soup or slightly drier so it will hold some shape in the bowl, suit yourself.

flavourings as desired – see side panel

BASIC RISOTTO

3 tbsp butter
1 small onion or 2 shallots, peeled and finely diced
finely grated zest of 1 lemon, no pith
2 cups arborio, Vialone Nano or other Italian risotto rice
½ cup dry white wine
6 cups good stock, eg chicken or vegetable, heated
salt and freshly ground black pepper
½ cup freshly grated parmesan

PREPARE desired flavourings (see side panel) and set aside. Melt butter in a heavy pot and gently cook onion and zest about 5 minutes or until onion is clear but not browned. Stir in rice over heat for another minute to lightly toast and coat the grains with butter. Add wine and cook until evaporated.

ADD all the hot stock. Stir well, season to taste and cover. Bring to a boil then lower the heat and put the timer on for 16 minutes. Stir occasionally and add more stock if the rice starts to get dry and stops looking like a soupy porridge.

AFTER rice has cooked 16 minutes, stir in mushrooms if using and more stock or water to return risotto to a sloppy, soupy texture. Stir through parmesan (the mixture should be very sloppy). Cover and cook another 5 minutes. Check seasoning and serve.

COOK'S NOTE: To check if the rice is cooked, use the back of a knife to crush one of the grains. The rice needs to be cooked until there is no longer a hard, white core at the centre. Start checking after 18 minutes.

ROSEMARY GRILLED TUNA ON GREEN BEAN NIÇOISE SALAD

MAKES: 6 serves PREP TIME: 10 minutes COOK TIME: 5 minutes
MAKE AHEAD: make dressing up to a week ahead and chill; marinate fish and prepare salad ingredients up to 8 hours ahead

ROSEMARY CHILLI OIL

Infused oils add an aromatic depth to marinades and dressings and also make a flavoursome garnish. You will need to heat the oil for coarse-leaved herbs such as rosemary and "wet" ingredients such as chillies or garlic, which (unless vinegar is added) need gentle cooking to evaporate the water in their cells (the water will cause fermentation).

Place ½ cup **rosemary leaves** (stripped off stalks) into a small pot with 2 **chillies**, halved lengthways (optional), and 1 cup **olive oil**. Heat very gently for about 6 minutes so the rosemary gently sizzles or bake in the oven at 150°C / 300°F for 15 minutes. Store in a clean jar. Oil will keep up to 2 months. Strain before use.

Fresh tuna is one of those serious food experiences – until you have tried it you can't imagine how any protein could have such a buttery, melt-in-the-mouth texture. This dish lends itself to all kinds of variations – you can use other types of fish or use a good quality canned fish and toss into the salad some lightly boiled baby potatoes, a few anchovy slivers, some hard-boiled quail eggs and baby spinach leaves. A little aioli dolloped on top of the fish is also particularly good.

4 steaks freshest tuna or other game fish

MARINADE	**¼ cup Rosemary Chilli Oil (see side panel) or extra virgin olive oil**
	finely grated zest of 1 lemon
	salt and freshly ground black pepper
NIÇOISE DRESSING	**2 small cloves garlic, crushed**
	3 semi-dried or sun-dried tomatoes, finely sliced
	¼ cup extra virgin olive oil
	2 tbsp lemon juice
	salt and freshly ground black pepper
	2 tbsp torn basil leaves or chopped parsley
	OPTIONAL: **1 anchovy, finely minced**
SALAD	**300g / 11oz baby French beans, trimmed**
	200g / 7oz cherry tomatoes, halved
	½ cup small niçoise or other tasty, small black olives
	2 tbsp tiny capers (nonpareils)

POUR oil over fish and mix through with lemon zest, salt and pepper. Cover and chill for 1-8 hours.

PLACE dressing ingredients in a jar, seal and shake well to combine. Drop beans into boiling water and cook 4 minutes, refresh under cold water and drain well. Place in a bowl with tomatoes, olives and capers. Toss with dressing. Season to taste.

LIFT fish out of marinade and grill 10cm / 4 inches from heat for 2-3 minutes each side or fry in a very hot pan or on a barbecue hot plate for about 1½ minutes each side until still pink in the centre (all game fish should be served slightly rare).
To serve, divide salad between serving plates and top with a piece of fish.

DESSERTS

Usually by the time dessert comes around everyone is relaxed, the room is full of animated chatter and laughter, and your skills as a talented cook are being celebrated. Flushed with success you may, quite justifiably, be about to hoover into the red wine. Before you slip into that bottle and under the table, hang on – it's not quite over yet. You may not feel like dessert but this is what everyone else has been waiting for – the moment their sybaritic fantasies can be appeased, a chance they can let go in spoonfuls of cream, pastry, chocolate and other forbidden dessert luxuries. They don't get this at home. In these weight-conscious times it's the ultimate treat.

It's your host bound duty to deliver this ritual high point to the meal. Whether you buy in / assemble / prepare from scratch is up to you. Deprive your guests entirely and there will be more than a few miffed mutterings in the car on the way home.

Unless you are a born performer I don't recommend the table-side flaming of crepes or noisy zabaglione whippings. Better to make dessert ahead of time and let it freeze or bake well before you need it. Have everything ready to go and enough for seconds so you can either plate up or let people help themselves. If your guests are all weight watchers then steer clear of the sticky date pudding, crème brûlée and double chocolate fudge brownie. Grilled fruit and yogurt or vanilla roasted peaches will do just nicely.

LEFT: Syrupy Grilled Fruits (recipe page 116)

know how

ITALIAN CUSTARD

The addition of mascarpone and lemon zest gives custard a distinctly Italian flavour. Use this wherever you might serve regular vanilla custard.

Whisk 200g / 7oz **mascarpone** and the finely grated zest of ¹/₂ small **lemon** into cooled **Vanilla Custard** (recipe on opposite page). Whisk until smooth. Place a piece of plastic wrap on top to stop a skin forming. Custard can be made in advance, kept chilled and reheated. Makes 3 cups.

WHIPPING CREAM

Cream doubles in volume when whipped. To achieve a silky smooth texture cream needs to be very cold when it is whipped and kept chilled until serving time. Whipped cream thickens up in the fridge so don't over-whip to start. If you have over-whipped cream you can fold in cold, runny cream to bring it back to a smooth texture. This works provided you haven't beaten the cream to the point where it has separated.

DESSERT TARTS

A cooked sweet pastry crust provides a vehicle for all kinds of alluring fillings. If you can't be bothered making your own pastry, use a good commercial brand. But really, you don't need a degree in astrophysics to make good pastry – just a set of measures and a food processor. This recipe makes enough to freeze in bulk for easy anytime use.

MELT-IN-THE-MOUTH SWEET PASTRY

MAKES: about 1kg / 2lb dough PREP TIME: 10 minutes plus 10 minutes chilling
COOK TIME: 20-35 minutes
MAKE AHEAD: chill dough up to 5 days or freeze up to 6 months; cooked pastry cases can be stored in an airtight container up to 5 days

This recipe comes from the kitchen of City Cake Company and features in "Sweet Indulgence", a book we collaborated on. It's simple to make and yields a consistently tender, crisp crust. The recipe makes a big amount – enough for 3 x 24cm / 9.5 inch tarts or 24 individual ones – so when I make it I divide it up and freeze the excess in blocks.

> 360g / 13 oz / 1¹/₂ cups butter, softened
> 185g / 1 cup less 2 tbsp sugar
> 1 egg
> 440g / 3¹/₃ cups flour
> pinch salt

BEAT BUTTER and sugar together until creamy and fluffy. Beat in egg. Add flour and salt and mix until just combined. Mixture will be soft. Using lightly floured hands, pat dough into 3 or more portions (pat between plastic wrap if desired). Use immediately or seal in plastic wrap and chill or freeze until required.

TO USE Roll dough on a lightly floured board or between 2 sheets of plastic wrap or teflon paper to 3mm / ¹/₈ inch thickness. Cut out pastry shapes to line individual muffin pans or pie dishes. Repair any cracks with extra pastry so you have a perfect shell. Chill for at least 10 minutes before baking. Alternatively, turn pastry into a shallow 23cm (9 inch) pie dish, removing plastic wrap and pressing out pastry to line the base and sides.

TO BAKE BLIND (to produce a cooked, unfilled pastry case): Preheat oven to 160°C / 325°F fan bake. Cover pastry with a piece of baking parchment or a double layer of foil that has been lightly sprayed with oil. Fill with dried beans or special pie weights. Bake 10-15 minutes, until pastry has just set. Remove paper and beans then bake a further 15-20 minutes or until shell is cooked through and a pale golden colour. Cool cases completely before filling.

RASPBERRY LIME CURD TARTS

Spoon Lime Curd into cooked, sweet pastry cases. Top with berries and dust with icing (confectioners') sugar.

LIME CURD

1 cup sugar ◇ 200g / 7oz unsalted butter, diced ◇ finely grated zest of 3 limes ◇ ½ cup lime juice ◇ 4 eggs, lightly beaten

Place all ingredients except eggs in a pot and bring to the boil. Remove mixture from heat and whisk in eggs. Place pot over a larger pot of boiling water (you will need a pot that the smaller one will fit on top of snugly) and stir constantly until sauce is thickened. Chill. Curd will keep 10 days. Makes 2 cups.

STRAWBERRY CUSTARD TARTS

This simple dessert is a last-minute assembly. Spoon cold Vanilla Custard or Italian Custard (recipe opposite page) into cooked, sweet pastry cases. Top with overlapping slices of fresh strawberries and brush over a little sieved raspberry jam to glaze.

VANILLA CUSTARD

2 cups milk ◇ 2 egg yolks ◇ ½ cup sugar ◇ 1 tbsp flour ◇ 1 tsp vanilla extract

Heat milk until small bubbles form around edge. Remove from heat. Beat egg yolks with sugar and flour until smooth. Whisk in hot milk. Transfer to a saucepan. Cook over medium heat, stirring constantly, until sauce comes to a simmer. Cook 1 minute longer then remove from heat and stir in vanilla.

SYRUPY GRILLED FRUITS
(PICTURED PAGE 112)

If you thought you'd run out of time to make dessert here's a fresh, speedy solution. Allow about 1½ **stone fruit** per person or use slices of **fresh pineapple** or **mango**. Place fruit in a baking dish lined with baking parchment. Drizzle each half with 1 tsp **Cardamom** and **Star Anise Syrup**. (page 118) or **maple syrup**.

Grill about 8-10cm / 4 inches from heat source until fruit has softened and started to brown around the edges. Serve warm or at room temperature drizzled with extra syrup and accompanied with ice cream or yogurt.

GRILLED PINEAPPLE

Cut slices of fresh golden pineapple. Sprinkle with **brown sugar** and a **splash of rum** **(optional)**. Leave for at least 5 minutes or up to 2 hours. Cook on a hot grill plate for a few minutes to lightly brown.

ROASTED PLUM TARTS

MAKES: 6 single-serve tarts PREP TIME: 10 minutes COOK TIME: 8-10 minutes
MAKE AHEAD: pastry can be cooked up to 48 hours ahead, plums up to 24 hours ahead and filling mixed together up to 24 hours ahead

A cooked, sweet pastry case forms the basis for all kinds of luxury fruit tarts. I tend to make a big batch of pastry and have it on hand in the freezer for ready access any time. This combination of tart plums, creamy filling and tender, crunchy pastry is utterly beguiling. Plum varieties vary in the amount of juice they will yield so if the ones you use don't get very juicy add a little more syrup as they grill.

6 individual baked sweet pastry shells made with Melt-in-the-Mouth
Sweet Pastry (page 114) or commercial sweet pastry

GLAZED PLUMS	9 plums (allow 1½ per tart) about ¼ cup maple syrup
FILLING	6 tbsp thick, creamy yogurt 3 tbsp thickened or whipped cream 2 tbsp icing (confectioners') sugar

HEAT oven to 250°C / 475°F. Halve plums and remove stones. Place fruit cut-side up on a shallow baking tray fully lined with tinfoil to hold the cooking juices. Drizzle with maple syrup. Bake 8-10 minutes or until plums are very slightly browned and juices have caramelised. Cool on the tray, then chill if desired for up to 24 hours.

FILLING In a bowl combine yogurt, cream and icing sugar. Cover and chill until ready to assemble tarts.

TO ASSEMBLE: Do this just before serving. Dollop a spoonful of cream filling into each cooked pastry shell. Top with 3 glazed plum halves and drizzle over the juices.

◇ VARIATIONS: Use other roasted fruit or a fresh fruit salad in place of the plums.

VELVET LEMON TART

SERVES: 10-12 PREP TIME: 10 minutes COOK TIME: about 1 hour plus standing time
MAKE AHEAD: on the morning of serving

Glenys Cennamo, who works with me in our test kitchen, came up with this utterly
divine version of the classic French dessert. If you can access thickened cream (which
contains a little gelatine) do use it as it does help to give the tart its impeccable
texture. Make this the day you plan to serve it – it tends to crack after a day or so.
Take particular care to check that the oven temperature is not too hot. It needs to set
the custard and no more.

Flavoured sugar syrups make a
terrific garnish for all kinds of
desserts and will keep for months
in the fridge.

Place in a pot 1½ cups **sugar**,
1 cup **water**, 6 whole **star anise**,
5-6 **cardamom pods**, roughly
crushed, and the peel of 1 **lemon**,
removed with a potato peeler
(no pith). Heat over medium heat,
stirring occasionally, until sugar
dissolves. Boil 5 minutes. Cool
and store in a sealed jar in the
refrigerator. Makes 1½ cups.

LEMON DESSERT SYRUP

Use ½ cup **lemon juice** and the
peel of 2 **lemons** in place of the
star anise and **cardamom**.

GINGER AND CINNAMON
DESSERT SYRUP

Use 20 thin slices of **fresh ginger**
and 3 **cinnamon sticks** in place of
the **star anise** and **cardamom**.

> 2 sheets sweet pastry (or ½ recipe Melt-in-the-Mouth Sweet Pastry)
>   (page 114)
> a little beaten egg

FILLING
> ⅔ cup fresh lemon juice
> 7 eggs, lightly beaten
> 1⅓ cups sugar
> 1¼ cups thickened or whipping cream

HEAT oven to 180°C / 350°F. Roll out pastry thinly to fit a 30cm / 12 inch flan dish,
covering base and sides. Cover with a sheet of baking parchment, spread pie weights
(I use dried beans) on top and bake 15 minutes.

REDUCE heat to 160°C / 325°F. Carefully remove paper and weights, brush pastry
with beaten egg and return to oven for a further 15 minutes or until golden and dry.

TO MAKE FILLING Combine all ingredients in a saucepan and warm very gently over
low heat until just lukewarm or 50°C / 120°F. Pour through a strainer into cooked
pastry case and bake at 130°C / 275°F for 25-30 minutes or until just set (it should be
just a little wobbly right in the centre when you take it from the oven). Stand at least
1 hour before serving.

GARNISH if desired with blackberries and a drizzle of Lemon Dessert Syrup (see panel
at left).

◇ LIME TART: Use ⅔ cup lime juice in place of the lemon juice.
◇ PASSIONFRUIT TART: Use ⅔ cup strained fresh passionfruit pulp in place
  of the lemon juice.

RUBY ROASTED PEARS

SERVES: 6 PREP TIME: 15 minutes COOK TIME: 30 minutes to poach, 20 minutes
to roast
MAKE AHEAD: poach pears up to 3 days before using, ready for a final roast

GREEK YOGURT
This is a delicious accompaniment
to a bowl of fresh fruit.

Fold together 250ml unsweetened
yogurt, 100ml sour cream and
2 tbsp liquid honey.

Keep chilled in a covered
container until ready to use.
Makes 1½ cups. It will keep for
up to a week in the fridge.

SPICED MASCARPONE
1½ cups mascarpone
2 tbsp icing (confectioners') sugar
finely grated zest of ½ lemon
1 tsp ground cinnamon
1 tsp lemon juice

Stir ingredients together until
evenly combined. Mixture will
keep 4-5 days in a covered
container in the fridge.

These pears are first poached and then roasted, which gives them a wonderfully
intense flavour and deep burnished hue. They taste best after being chilled in their
liquid for up to 3 days before roasting so they can absorb the flavours and colour of
the syrup.

> 2 cups sugar
> 3 cups red wine
> 3 cinnamon sticks
> 4 bay leaves
> 1 vanilla pod
> 6 just-ripe pears with stems intact

CHOOSE a pot that will fit 6 pears snugly upright in a single layer. Heat sugar, wine,
cinnamon sticks, bay leaves and vanilla pod, stirring until sugar has dissolved.

PEEL pears, leaving whole with stalks intact, and place in pot, arranging so they are
all covered as much as possible by the syrup. Simmer gently for 30 minutes or until
tender, turning occasionally.

COOL pears then place with their syrup in a container, cover and chill for at least 24
hours or up to 3 days, turning occasionally to colour evenly.

LIFT pears out of syrup and arrange in a shallow baking dish. On top of the stove, fast
boil syrup until reduced by half. Remove bay leaves, cinnamon and vanilla pod.

TO SERVE: Heat oven to 200°C / 400°F. Baste pears with syrup to coat and roast for
20 minutes. Brush with more syrup as they come out of the oven. Place on serving
plates with a large spoonful of syrup. Accompany with Spiced Mascarpone (see side
panel).

COOK'S NOTE: Rinse and dry the vanilla pod after preparing this recipe, then store
it in a coffee or sugar jar to use again.

menu 6

MERINGUES

MAKES: about 150 tiny meringues or about 70 medium-sized ones
PREP TIME: 15 minutes COOK TIME: 1 hour plus cooling
MAKE AHEAD: these need to be made at least a day ahead and will keep for several
weeks in an airtight container

I used to think that my mother's meringues were the best known to mankind but these
ones with icing (confectioners') sugar folded through offer even more of an exquisite
collapse with a heavenly, chewy centre. The recipe makes oodles of meringues but they
keep for weeks in a sealed container and are incredibly useful to pull out for an
emergency dessert. Don't make them on a humid day.

> 5 large egg whites (175g / 6 oz)
> pinch salt
> 160g / 6oz caster (superfine) sugar
> 160g / 6oz icing (confectioners') sugar
> 1 tsp vanilla extract

HEAT oven to 180°C / 350°F. In a very clean bowl and using an electric beater, beat
egg whites with salt until stiff. Add caster sugar and beat on high speed for 10
minutes. Fold in icing sugar and vanilla.

SPOON tiny spoonfuls of mixture onto baking trays lined with baking parchment.
Place trays in preheated oven and immediately turn heat down to 120°C / 250°F. Cook
1 hour. Turn off oven and leave meringues to cool in oven.

TO SERVE: sandwich meringues with whipped cream up to an hour before serving.

◇ OTHER SERVING IDEAS: Sandwich meringues with flavoured whipped cream,
  eg mix in lime curd (page 115), berry compote (page 131), passionfruit pulp or
  Kahlua liqueur. Dust lightly with sieved cocoa if desired.

know how

PERFECTING PAVLOVA

Pavlova is a favourite New Zealand dessert. It tastes and has a texture similar to a cross between meringue and marshmallow, and is traditionally served with whipped cream, kiwifruit and passionfruit. If you wish to maintain its low-fat virtues serve pavlova with fresh berries and the Mixed Berry Compote on page 131.

INDIVIDUAL COCONUT PAVLOVAS
MAKES: 6-8 individual pavlovas PREP TIME: 15-20 minutes
COOK TIME: 1 hour, plus cooling
MAKE AHEAD: store in an airtight container up to 5 days or freeze

The basic pavlova mixture of egg whites, sugar, cornflour (cornstarch) and vinegar can be flavoured in many ways. Ground almonds or hazelnuts, coffee or cocoa are popular additions as is coconut, which features here. Whatever flavour you choose, stir it gently into the meringue right at the end. Don't beat it in as any oils in the flavouring will deflate the delicate structure of the meringue.

> 4 egg whites, preferably not too fresh, at room temperature
> pinch salt
> 1 cup caster (superfine) sugar
> 1 tsp cornflour (cornstarch)
> 1/2 tsp malt vinegar
> 3/4 cup coarse thread coconut, plus a little extra for sprinkling

HEAT oven to 180°C / 350°F and line a baking tray with baking parchment. Place egg whites in the bowl of an electric mixer. Add salt and beat to soft peaks. Slowly add sugar with the beater running. Beat 10 minutes or until mixture is shiny and glossy and very thick. Whisk in cornflour and vinegar then fold in coconut.

USE a large spoon to place 6-8 dollops of mixture on the baking tray. Swirl tops with a fork or spatula. Bake 3 minutes then reduce oven temperature to 120°C / 250°F and cook 1 hour or until pavlova shells are crisp to the touch. Turn off oven and leave to cool in oven. Store in an airtight container.

TO SERVE: Top meringues with Mango Passionfruit Topping (see opposite page) or any other topping of your choice.

SOFT MERINGUE ROULADE
Prepare pavlova recipe as at right (omitting the coconut) up to the point where it is ready to take out of the bowl.

Heat oven to 180°C / 350°F. Line a baking tray with parchment and mark out a rectangle about 35cm x 24cm / 14 x 10 inches. Spread meringue to fill rectangle to an even thickness of about 1.5cm / 1/2 inch. Bake 7-8 minutes or until meringue has just set. Take out of oven and invert at once onto a clean tea towel dusted with 1/2 cup icing (confectioners') sugar and 1/2 cup toasted sliced almonds. (Holding on to the paper will make this feat easier.) Cool, cover and chill up to 48 hours.
Spread with whipped cream, passionfruit cream, Chocolate Mousse (opposite page) or other flavoured cream of your choice and roll up gently along longest edge. Chill before carefully transferring to a serving plate, joined edge down. Keep chilled until ready to serve. Serve in slices. Serves 8-10.

MANGO PASSIONFRUIT TOPPING

This is a delicious dessert topping. You could also garnish the pavlovas with berries or diced kiwifruit.

◇ 1½ cups chilled whipping cream
◇ 1 tbsp icing (confectioners') sugar
1 tsp vanilla extract ◇ ½ cup passionfruit pulp or syrup ◇ flesh of 1 peeled mango or ¼ fresh pineapple, thinly sliced

Whip cream to soft peaks with sugar and vanilla. Fold in ¼ cup passionfruit pulp. Dollop onto each pavlova, top with sliced fruit and drizzle over remaining passionfruit pulp.

CHOCOLATE MOUSSE FILLING

This makes a decadent filling for meringue roulade (pictured right) or can be served as a mousse with berries.

Break up **100g / 3½ oz dark chocolate** and heat with ¼ **cup cream** for 1 minute in the microwave or in a pan over hot water. Stir until smooth. Cool.
Whip ¾ **cup cold cream** to firm peaks and fold into chocolate. Cover and chill until firm, about 1 hour.

MACAROON TOPPING FOR PEACHES OR PIES

This sweet, gooey macaroon topping is sensational. Bake it on top of peach halves, or mix with fresh raspberries for an amazing tart filling. The recipe evolved from Maury Rubin's excellent Book of Tarts.

12-16 fresh ripe peach halves, eg Golden Queen

Macaroon topping
1 cup cream
1 cup sugar
4 cups coarse thread coconut
1/2 tsp vanilla extract

Heat cream and sugar until it boils and sugar has dissolved. Remove from heat and mix in coconut and vanilla. Allow to cool. Pile on to peach halves and bake at 160°C / 325°F for 45 minutes or until peaches are soft and topping is golden. Serves 6-8.

MACAROON RASPBERRY TARTS

Mix about 1½ cups raspberries (fresh or frozen) into cooled macaroon topping mixture and pile into 8 pre-cooked sweet tart cases. Bake at 160°C / 325°F for 30 minutes or until lightly golden.

VANILLA-ROASTED PEACHES

SERVES: 6 PREP TIME: 10 minutes COOK TIME: 30-40 minutes
MAKE AHEAD: peaches can be cooked 6-8 hours ahead and reheated gently before serving

This is an incredibly simple idea, yet the flavours produced are rich and luscious. Make these when summer stone fruit are in peak supply. Here I've served the peaches on custard and scattered fresh raspberries around. You could also serve them with ice cream, yogurt or whipped cream.

> 6 fresh, ripe peaches, nectarines or other stone fruit (unpeeled)
> 1 vanilla pod, split in half lengthways and each half cut into 3 pieces
> 1/2 cup fruity wine such riesling, or water
> 1/4 cup sugar
>
> GARNISH: Chilled Vanilla Custard or Italian Custard (page 114)
>   and fresh raspberries
> icing (confectioners') sugar to dust

HEAT oven to 200°C / 400°F. Make a shallow cross in the top of each fruit and insert a strip of vanilla. Place fruit in a small roasting dish, pour over wine or water and sprinkle with sugar. Roast 30-40 minutes or until tender.

TO SERVE: Spoon a pool of custard onto each serving plate. Top with fruit and spoon over cooking syrup. Scatter raspberries around and dust with icing sugar.

CREAMY SEMIFREDDO

Make this simple ice cream up to 3 weeks ahead and freeze. Once thawed don't refreeze it for food safety reasons.

3 eggs
2 egg yolks
1 cup caster (superfine) sugar
2 tsp vanilla extract
2 cups whipping cream

Place eggs, yolks and sugar in a stainless steel bowl. Place over a saucepan of simmering water and whisk constantly for 5 minutes or until mixture is very frothy and heated right through. Remove from heat and beat with an electric mixer for 5 minutes or until mixture is thickened and pale. Gradually mix in vanilla on low speed. Beat cream to soft peaks. Fold egg mixture into cream.Pour into serving cups or a plastic container. Cover and freeze for at least 8 hours.

GINGER PASSION SEMIFREDDO

Mix 2 tsp ground ginger and 150g finely chopped glacé ginger into prepared ice cream mixture before freezing.

MACADAMIA AND WHITE CHOCOLATE SEMIFREDDO

Mix 120g chopped white chocolate and 120g chopped macadamia nuts into ice cream mixture before freezing.

RHUBARB AND APPLE CRUMBLE

SERVES: 8-10 PREP TIME: 10 minutes COOK TIME: 45 minutes
MAKE AHEAD: can be assembled ready to cook and refrigerated for several hours before cooking; crumble mixture can be made in bulk and stored in the fridge or freezer for a speedy dessert

Use fresh or canned fruit as available and play around with the flavours – peach or pear and ginger crumble, tamarillo or redcurrant and apple, rhubarb and berry. If the fruit is very wet sift 1-2 teaspoons cornflour (cornstarch) over it and mix through before topping with crumble.

2 cups cooked apples or 567g / 20oz can apples
3 stalks rhubarb, chopped into 2.5cm / 1 inch pieces
1/4 cup sugar

CRUMBLE TOPPING
1 cup flour
1 cup brown sugar
1 1/2 cups rolled oats, finest cut available
1 cup coarse thread coconut
1 tsp ground ginger
50g / 2oz chopped almonds
140g / 2/3 cup butter, melted

HEAT oven to 160°C / 325°F. Place apples and rhubarb in a large (30-35cm / 12-14 inch), shallow baking dish and sprinkle with sugar. Combine topping ingredients and spread evenly over fruit. Bake 40-45 minutes or until golden. Accompany with Vanilla or Italian Custard (page 114), whipped cream or Creamy Semifreddo (see side panel).

◇ VARIATION: Almond Crumble Topping. Use 1/2 cup ground almonds in place of 1/2 cup rolled oats in crumble mixture.

RIGHT: Rhubarb and Apple Crumble with Vanilla Custard.

SWEET SAUCES

Use a good quality commercial ice cream or make your own fabulous semifreddo – see recipe previous page. Either way, ice cream gets a stylish lift with a smart sauce.

AMARETTO COFFEE SYRUP
Heat 1 cup very strong espresso coffee with ³/₄ cup sugar in a small pot, stirring to dissolve sugar. Boil 8-10 minutes or until reduced by about a third. Mix in 2 tsp lemon juice and ¹/₄ cup Amaretto liqueur or other liqueur of your choice. Cool, transfer to a clean container, cover and store in the fridge. Syrup will keep for weeks. Makes 1 cup.

CARAMEL SAUCE
A useful make-ahead sauce, this keeps for about a week in the fridge.

Place 1 cup cream, 1 cup brown sugar, ¹/₄ cup golden syrup (light corn syrup) and 1 tsp vanilla extract in a pan and stir over heat until sugar has dissolved. Boil 5 minutes or until slightly reduced and a rich brown colour.

WICKED CHOCOLATE SAUCE
Heat 2 cups cream and mix in 250g / ¹/₂ lb dark chocolate, broken into small bits, until melted. Stir in 2 tbsp Kahlua or other liqueur of your choice. Cool, transfer to a clean container, cover and store in the fridge. Sauce will keep for 4-5 days. Reheat to soften for serving. Makes 3 cups.

MIXED BERRY COMPOTE
With its intense berry flavour, this sauce is one of those really useful standbys to have in the fridge. Use it as a topping for ice cream, grilled fruits or pavlova, either alone as a fat-free option or mixed into whipped cream or mascarpone.

In a stainless steel pot place 3 cups mixed frozen berries, ¹/₄ cup water, 1 cup sugar, 1 tsp vanilla extract and 1 bay leaf (optional). Bring to the boil then reduce heat and simmer 15 minutes. Lift out bay leaf. Add ¹/₄ cup kirsch if desired. Cool, transfer to a clean container, cover and store in the fridge. Sauce will keep for several weeks and reheats well. Makes 2 cups.

GINGER MANGO PASSION SAUCE
Light and fresh with the zing of ginger. Great for ice cream or to partner a fresh fruit salad.
Purée 425g / 15oz can mangoes in juice until smooth. Mix in 1 tsp grated fresh ginger, 1 tsp maple syrup or sugar and the strained flesh of 2-3 passionfruit or 2-3 tbsp preserved passionfruit in syrup. Transfer to a clean container, cover and store in the fridge. Sauce will keep 3-4 days. Makes 1³/₄ cups.

LEFT: Caramel Sauce with Creamy Semifreddo (page 128) and Grilled Pineapple (page 114).

VANILLA PANNA COTTA WITH GREEN FRUIT SALAD

SERVES: 6-8 PREP TIME: 15 minutes COOK TIME: 6-8 minutes plus at least 4 hours to set MAKE AHEAD: panna cotta can be made up to 48 hours ahead (cover tightly); fruit salad can be made up to 4 hours ahead

This combination of silky cream and fresh fruit wins rave reviews, and the sweet spike of praline adds a sublime finishing touch for a special occasion. Cream takes well to a multitude of flavourings – ginger, almond oil, rosewater, cardamom, lime and orange are some flavours you may like to try, but I find it hard to go past vanilla. Here I have served some with a luscious fruit salad and others with fresh raspberries and blueberries.

ALMOND PRALINE

Make this toffee with any kind of nut and use it to flavour ice creams and sauces or as a garnish.

1 cup caster (superfine) sugar
2 tbsp water
75g sliced almonds (or other nuts)

Line a shallow baking tray with baking parchment or grease with oil. Place sugar and water in a saucepan over low heat. Stir just until sugar has dissolved. Bring to the boil without stirring, brushing down sides of pot with water to prevent crystals forming. Cook 2-3 minutes or until syrup turns a rich gold. Add nuts and pour at once into lined tray, tilting to spread out thinly. Cool then crush or break into shards. Store in an airtight container.

3 level tsp gelatine
2 tbsp cold water
2 cups cream
1 cup milk
1 tsp vanilla extract
$^1/_3$ cup caster (superfine) sugar
OPTIONAL GARNISH: **Almond Praline - see side panel**

GREEN FRUIT SALAD
$^1/_3$ honeydew melon, peeled, seeded and cut into small chunks
250g / 9oz seedless green grapes
4 kiwifruit, peeled and cut in chunks
$^1/_4$ cup Ginger and Cinnamon Dessert Syrup – page 118
OPTIONAL ADDITIONS: **canned lychees, poached figs**

MIX gelatine with water so it is fully absorbed and there are no dry bits. Set aside. Place cream, milk, vanilla and sugar in a saucepan and slowly bring to the boil. As soon as it bubbles, remove from the heat. Whisk in gelatine, making sure it has fully dissolved. Cool mixture slightly then divide between 6-8 serving glasses. Chill until set.

PREPARE fruit and chill in a covered container until ready to serve.

TO SERVE: Divide fruit between glasses of panna cotta, drizzle syrup over and sprinkle with praline.

RIGHT: Panna Cotta with Green Fruit Salad and fresh berries, garnished with Almond Praline.

132

NAUGHTY TARTE TATIN

So easy and so good – a gooey pudding that deserves lashings of whipped cream.

1/4 cup sugar
2 tbsp golden syrup (light corn syrup)
1 tbsp butter
2 tbsp marmalade
1kg / 2 lb cooking apples, peeled, cored and sliced in sixths (or use canned apple slices)
juice of 1/2 lemon
250g puff pastry

Heat sugar, golden syrup, butter and marmalade in a medium-large, heavy ovenproof pan or paella dish, stirring until sugar has fully dissolved.

Arrange apples in a single overlapping pattern in pan. Cook until apples are semi-tender and coated with caramel. This will take about 25 minutes (10 minutes less for canned apples). There should not be any excess watery liquid in the pan. Remove from heat. (Dish can be prepared to this point and chilled ahead of time.)

Heat oven to 200°C / 400°F.

Roll out pastry to fit top of pan. Place over apples, leaving edge unsealed, and cut 3 slits in the top. Bake 20 minutes or until pastry is golden.

To serve, invert tart onto a large, flat serving plate. Serves 6.

STICKY GINGER DATE PUDDING WITH CARAMEL SAUCE

SERVES: 6-8 PREP TIME: 10 minutes plus cooling COOK TIME: 30 minutes
MAKE AHEAD: cooked puddings can be frozen then thawed and gently heated in the microwave for 2 minutes or a warm oven for 10 minutes before serving. Caramel sauce can be made up to 5 days ahead and chilled.

This nostalgic winter pudding is inspired by Stephanie Alexander's sticky toffee pudding. It adapts well to variations such as prunes instead of dates or finely grated lemon zest in place of ginger. I sometimes add the diced flesh of 2 pears to the batter before cooking.

> 300ml / 1 1/4 cups boiling water
> 200g / 7oz dates, chopped
> 60g / 4 tbsp butter
> 3/4 tsp baking soda (be careful not to use more than this or it will leave a taste)
> 3/4 cup brown sugar
> 1/4 cup golden syrup
> 2 eggs, room temperature
> 1 tsp vanilla extract
> 1 1/3 cups / 200g / 7oz flour
> 1 tsp baking powder
> 50g / 1 1/2oz crystallised ginger, finely chopped
> TO SERVE: **Caramel Sauce (page 131) and crème fraîche, or Greek yogurt (page 120)**

HEAT oven to 180°C / 350°F and grease 6 large (Texas) muffin tins or 8 medium muffin pans or a 24cm / 8 inch square baking tin. (To help the easy removal of the puddings I line each muffin pan with a long strip of baking parchment so the ends overhang.)

POUR the boiling water over dates and butter and stir to melt butter. Mix in baking soda and leave to cool completely. Stir in brown sugar and golden syrup until evenly combined. Add eggs and vanilla and stir well.

GENTLY fold in flour, baking powder and ginger (it will be a very wet mixture, don't over-mix). Pour into prepared tins and bake about 30 minutes.

CHECK pudding is cooked by inserting a skewer into the middle – it should come out clean. Turn out and serve with hot Caramel Sauce. Top with a dollop of crème fraîche.

ARGENTINE FLAN

SERVES: 8 PREP TIME: 10 minutes COOK TIME: 45-50 minutes
MAKE AHEAD: needs to be made at least 8 hours ahead and will keep in the fridge
up to 2 days

In the early 1980s I lived for nearly a year in the coastal resort of Buzios, north of Rio. It was here I started my first food business, making croissants. My playmates were, for the most part, Argentines in exile. From these old friends comes this light, caramelly dessert – it's a classic in their country and, unlike its French equivalent, does not contain cream.

$^1/_2$ cup sugar
1$^1/_2$ tbsp water
4 cups milk
3 tbsp sugar
5 eggs
1 tsp vanilla extract
GARNISH: **2 finely diced kiwifruit or 1 cup other**
    chopped fruit or berries

HEAT oven to 150°C / 300°F. Heat the first quantity of sugar with water in a small pot until it forms a rich, golden caramel. Remove from heat and pour into 8 lightly oiled, small muffin cups or ramekins (use a flavourless or sweet oil such as grapeseed or almond).

HEAT milk with second measure of sugar until dissolved and remove from heat. Lightly whisk eggs and vanilla until just combined (do not over-beat). Mix into hot milk. Strain mixture into prepared cups.

PLACE in a deep roasting dish filled with hot water to come halfway up the sides of the dishes. Bake 45-50 minutes or until custards are set and very lightly browned on top. Remove from water bath and leave to cool. Cover and chill at least 8 hours or up to 2 days.

TAKE out of the fridge half an hour before serving. Slide a knife around edge to loosen and turn out onto serving plates. Garnish with finely diced kiwifruit, orange segments, melon balls or raspberries.

menu 3

WHITE CHOCOLATE AND RASPBERRY PARFAIT

SERVES: 10-12 PREP TIME: 15 minutes COOK TIME: 2-3 minutes
MAKE AHEAD: parfait will keep for 3-4 weeks in a tightly covered container in the freezer

Fabulously glam yet a cinch to prepare. You'll need an electric beater for the base meringue. If preferred, freeze the parfait in individual moulds. Here I have frozen the parfait in 1 large container and used a cookie cutter to shape individual portions.

250g white chocolate, chopped
1/2 cup cream
4 large egg whites
1/3 cup caster sugar
1 tsp vanilla extract
2 tbsp lemon juice
1-1 1/2 cups raspberries, fresh or frozen (1 punnet = 1 cup)
TO SERVE: Liqueur Syrup (see below) and chopped pistachios

LINE the base and long sides of a 6-cup loaf pan or triangle mould with plastic wrap or paper lunchwrap, leaving an overhang on either side so that the frozen mixture can be easily lifted from the container.

PLACE chocolate and cream in a pot and gently warm 1-2 minutes or until the chocolate has softened. Stir to fully melt chocolate then remove from heat and cool.

USING a very clean electric beater, beat egg whites while gradually adding sugar. Beat until mixture forms stiff peaks.

ADD chocolate mixture to beaten egg whites along with vanilla and lemon juice. Fold gently to combine. At the very last minute fold in berries. Pour mixture into prepared tin. Cover with plastic wrap and freeze at least 6 hours or until solid.

SERVE with a spoonful of liqueur syrup and garnished with finely chopped pistachios.

| LIQUEUR | 1/2 cup maple syrup |
| SYRUP | 1/4 cup Cointreau or other liqueur of your choice |

MIX together and store in a sealed container in the fridge. Syrup will keep for months. Makes 3/4 cup.

◇ COCONUT, MACADAMIA AND PINEAPPLE PARFAIT: Instead of berries, fold 1 cup lightly toasted thread coconut, 3/4 cup finely chopped glacé pineapple and 1/2 cup chopped, toasted macadamia nuts into prepared parfait mixture before freezing.

QUICK BERRY DESSERTS

BERRY FOOL

Purée 2 cups raspberries with 2 tbsp icing (confectioners') sugar. Swirl through 2 cups chilled cream whipped to soft peaks. Chill before serving.

BERRY JELLY

Soften 5 tsp gelatine in 1/3 cup cold water. Heat 3 cups cranberry juice. Mix in gelatine to dissolve. Fill dessert cups with berries. Pour over juice to cover and chill until set.

AFTER DINNER INDULGENCES

At the end of a wonderful meal, indulge in a little treat to round things off.

COFFEE

You don't need a fancy espresso machine to make great coffee, just good quality beans that have been freshly ground. I use a stove-top Italian espresso boiler. A nip of whisky or other spirit is good after dinner, in which case offer a little bowl of whipped cream. And don't forget some good quality sugar crystals. Offer herbal teas as an alternative to coffee – ginger, chamomile and vanilla are all good, caffeine-free digestives.

PISTACHIO AND CHERRY CHOCOLATE SLICE

Hazelnuts and dried apricots are another good combination for this rich chocolate treat.

Place 350g / 12oz chopped, dark, good eating chocolate and 3/4 cup sweetened condensed milk in a large microwave bowl. Cook on high power for about 2 minutes, stirring every 30 seconds until melted and smooth. Mix in 2 tsp vanilla extract, 1/4 cup icing (confectioners') sugar, 1 cup roughly chopped glacé cherries and 3/4 cup shelled pistachios. Mixture will be very thick. Press into a small loaf pan lined with plastic wrap. Chill until set then store in a cool place. Makes about 30 slices.

CHEESE PLATTER

Cheese can be served as a substitute for dessert or as a separate course before dessert. Choose 2-3 generous wedges of ripe cheeses – a fragrant little goats' cheese, an oozy, mouthwateringly and slightly smelly washed rind cheese or brie, and perhaps a piece of aged hard cheese or a blue. Ensure cheeses are ripe and at room temperature when you serve them – take them out of the refrigerator a good hour before serving. Accompany with bread, seasonal fruits such as pears, grapes or figs, fruit pastes or muscatels.

A LATE NIGHT TIPPLE

The fine, clear taste of a well made fruit spirit, brandy or cognac offers a light digestive (according to the Italians anyway). My favourite is Poire Williams made with pears, but it's a hit of neat, pure alcohol that many people won't enjoy. Some people like port or sweet liquers such as Frangelico or Tia Maria. Dessert wines are another good ending option. The extraordinary flavours of chilled botrytised riesling or Sauternes is a delicious way to fill the palate at the end of a glorious meal.

ONE STEP CHOCOLATE CAKE

MAKES: 1 large cake to serve 12-16 people PREP TIME: 5 minutes COOK TIME: 1 hour
MAKE AHEAD: cake will keep fresh in a sealed container in the fridge for about a week, or can be frozen uniced

Thanks again to Glenys Cennamo for this terrific recipe. It's so incredibly simple – a magical conjuring up – as, without really needing to be at all clever, you get this huge, rich, dark, moist cake that's fabulous when you need a celebration cake in a hurry. If I am feeling reckless I melt a big block of chocolate with an equal measure of cream and slather it over the top.

2 cups sugar
2 large eggs
1 cup milk or unsweetened yoghurt
$3/4$ cup premium quality cocoa powder
200g (7oz) butter, softened
2 tsp baking soda
$1^1/2$ tsp vanilla extract
$1/4$ tsp salt
3 cups self-raising flour
1 cup boiling hot coffee
OPTIONAL GANACHE TOPPING: 250g / 8oz chocolate,
1 cup cream

HEAT oven to 160°C / 325°F and line a 30cm / 12 inch round cake tin with baking parchment. Place all ingredients in the bowl of a food processor and blitz until combined (or place ingredients in a mixing bowl and beat with an electric beater). Pour mixture into prepared tin and smooth the top. Bake for 1 hour or until a skewer inserted into the centre comes out clean. Cool in tin. Place in a sealed container or freeze if not using at once.

TO MAKE ganache, melt chocolate and cream over low heat in a pot or microwave for $1^1/2$-2 minutes, stirring every 30 seconds until chocolate is fully melted and mixture is creamy. Either drizzle from a spoon over the cake or cool ganache until it is firm enough to spread and cover cake.

OTHER SERVING SUGGESTIONS:
◇ Dust cake with icing (confectioners') sugar.
◇ Drizzle with Berry Compote (page 131) and serve with whipped cream.
◇ Split cake into 3 layers and spread each with raspberry jam. Reassemble and ice with chocolate ganache.

LEFT: One Step Chocolate Cake with ganache and raspberries

MENU PLANNING

Planning a menu always takes time. You think about the occasion, the people who are coming and what they might enjoy eating, about what's in season and what you like to cook. You wonder about the logistics of oven space, cooking temperatures and pots and pans as well as getting everything to the table cooked perfectly at the right time. And then you can't decide.

Don't make life hard for yourself with acts of last-minute culinary juggling. There are few things more disconcerting for a guest than to discover one's host howling in the kitchen over a botched risotto.

Build your menu around the main course, considering the cooking style in relation to the occasion. For example, if you are feeding a crowd a central main course dish is the most manageable strategy. Think about the weather and the season – when it's icy outside no one will want to eat chicken salad.

Build a starter and a dessert around the main, avoiding repeats both in ingredients and in texture – don't serve creamy sauced mains with creamy desserts. Make a schedule detailing what can be done ahead, what's needed at the last minute and checking you won't end up on the day needing the oven at the same time for two dishes that need to be cooked at different temperatures.

The following menus are all three-course events for special occasions. At all other times keep things simple with a main course and perhaps one of the simple assembly starters. Buy or make a dessert ahead of time and remember, everyone is coming to share a good time.

PLATTER OF FENNEL
SALAD, TUNA TARTARE
AND ROASTED STUFFED
CAPSICUMS

MEDITERRANEAN
STUFFED SALMON
FILLETS WITH LIME
HOLLANDAISE

FLASH-ROASTED CHERRY
TOMATOES, THYME
ROASTED BABY
POTATOES, GREEN BEANS

ROASTED PLUM TARTS

menu plan

Here's a menu that pulls out all the stops for a smart Saturday night dress-up dinner. It's just the sort of light, elegant fare to serve for a special birthday or to impress clients or colleagues. Pretty well everything can be prepared ahead of time so that when it comes to serving, the job is mainly assembly and final cooking. If fennel is out of season you could serve marinated olives instead, or make the baba ghanoush on page 14 and serve it spooned in to witloof or radicchio leaves.

In colder weather, serve Leek, Potato and Roasted Garlic Soup with breadsticks as a starter and Sticky Ginger Date Pudding for dessert.

ADVANCE PREPARATIONS

WELL AHEAD
DESSERT- Make pastry and chill or freeze. Bake pastry cases and store in airtight container.

DAY BEFORE
STARTER- Make fennel salad and chill. Roast capsicums.
MAIN- Make hollandaise and chill.
DESSERT- Mix dessert filling and chill.

ON THE DAY
STARTER- Make tuna tartare and chill.
MAIN- Stuff salmon and chill. Prepare vegetables and par cook potatoes (pages 64 and 91).
DESSERT- Roast plums.

FINAL PREPARATIONS
STARTER- Complete fennel salad and tuna tartare (adding lemon juice to each) and assemble plates.

MAIN- Complete potatoes, complete and cook salmon, timing it to go into the oven after the potatoes have cooked for 30 minutes. Warm hollandaise, cook beans and tomatoes.

DESSERT- Assemble just before serving.

WINE- Serve a chilled pinot gris with the starter, a buttery chardonnay with the salmon, and a sticky dessert wine with the tarts.

SPIKED PRAWN COCKTAIL OR PLATTER OF DELI NIBBLES

FISH CURRY, FRAGRANT RICE AND POPPADOMS

ICE CREAM WITH GRILLED PINEAPPLE AND CARAMEL SAUCE

The success of impromptu entertaining relies on a well stocked pantry and ready supplies of fresh vegetables. The last thing you want to be confronted with when unexpected guests turn up is a science experiment of dead, limp food in the fridge. Keep a stash of flavoursome pestos, dressings, sauces, dips and spreads in the fridge and some quick cooking premium proteins – lamb racks, chicken fillets, prawns – and pastry in the freezer.

One-dish meals are probably the easiest way to go here – a fresh, spicy South Indian style fish curry (featured here) or the Thai chicken curry, a big bowl of pasta or a creamy risotto. Partner with a fresh salad and bread and finish with ice cream and a sauce and you have a remarkably effortless execution and a very satisfying result. Fruity crumble or a naughty tarte tatin are a couple of other good impromptu desserts.

ADVANCE PREPARATIONS

WELL AHEAD
STARTER- Check freezer is stocked with prawns. Have Vietnamese dressing made and stored in the fridge.
MAIN- Store freshly frozen fish (or buy fresh fish on the day).
DESSERT- Have ice cream on hand in the freezer and caramel sauce made in the fridge (it will keep about a week).

DAY BEFORE
MAIN- Make the base for the curry and chill.

FINAL PREPARATIONS
STARTER- Assemble starter.

MAIN- Finish cooking curry, cook rice, beans and follow packet instructions for poppadoms.

DESSERT- Grill pineapple, warm sauce in pot or microwave.

WINE- Sauvignon blanc or pinot gris with the starter, riesling or gewürztraminer with the curry, bubbles if you like for dessert.

menu plan ②

PROSCIUTTO FIG SALAD

TWICE-ROASTED FIVE
SPICE DUCK

ARGENTINE FLAN

menu plan ③

There are two kinds of eaters in the world. Neophobic types are totally averse to any new tastes. They would possibly prefer to eat whatever childhood food their mother cooked them for the rest of their lives. Bring out the steak and kidney, please.

The neophiliacs sit at the opposite end of the spectrum, ready to embrace the next new dish, their curiosity piqued by vintages of balsamic vinegar and varieties of artichoke. Their adventurous palates are at the ready, craving the next great taste.

Autumn is one of the best times to stage a foodie dinner. The season's harvests peak in flavour and good things like figs and ducks fatten sweetly. If you are up to an extra course here, throw in Richard Harris' seared squid salad (page 41) – its light, spicy flavours go well between the fig salad and the duck. There are lots of options you could take with the dessert. If you feel like spending more time in the kitchen a platter of tastes would be sensational – vanilla-roasted peach, ginger semifreddo and cream-filled meringues.

ADVANCE PREPARATIONS

WELL AHEAD
STARTER- Make balsamic dressing.

DAY BEFORE
STARTER- Wash and dry salad greens and chill in plastic bag.
MAIN- Marinate duck.
DESSERT- Make flan and chill (it will keep up to 2 days in fridge provided it is tightly wrapped to prevent any fridge taint).

ON THE DAY
STARTER- Grill figs.
MAIN- Cook duck to end of first high heat stage.
DESSERT- Prepare kiwifruit and chill.

FINAL PREPARATIONS
STARTER- Assemble salad.

MAIN- Complete cooking duck, cook noodles and greens.

DESSERT- Take dessert out of fridge 30 minutes before serving.

WINE- Serve a dry riesling or pinot gris with the salad, a pinot noir with the duck and botrytised chilled riesling with the flan.

p42 : p88 : p90 : p134

SMOKED SALMON AND BREAD, FRESH OYSTERS OR SPICED ALMONDS

LAMB SHANKS WITH MASH, PEAS AND BEANS AND TOSSED GREEN SALAD

STICKY GINGER DATE PUDDING WITH CARAMEL SAUCE

A central star 'cook ahead' dish supported by bread, mash or roast vegetables and salad is the easiest way to feed a crowd.
Put out a stack of plates, cutlery and condiments and let people help themselves.

Avoid panicking about whether there will be enough food by doing a little pre-planning on numbers. Extend recipes accordingly and cook a little more than you think you will need. Have back-ups of bread and salad options you can pull out if unexpected extras turn up.

Braised oxtails with red chilli beans, chicken pie, fragrant lamb tagine and spicy chicken tagine are other good winter dishes that reheat well and can be made in bulk for a crowd.
In summer Thai chicken curry, fish and scallop pie, Asian chicken salad, or duck and mango salad are all good main course dishes that can be made in bulk.
One Step Chocolate Cake is a good dessert option that can be made ahead and frozen. Thaw the day of serving and ice with chocolate ganache.

ADVANCE PREPARATIONS

WELL AHEAD
STARTER- Make bread dough and chill or freeze (or buy bread). Make salad dressing. Buy a small side of hot smoked salmon or other smoked fish up to 2-3 days ahead and chill.
MAIN- Cook lamb shanks, chill and de-fat. Freeze if not using within 2 days.
DESSERT- Make caramel sauce.

ON THE DAY
STARTER- Cook bread, make horseradish cream if serving smoked salmon.
MAIN- Make mash.
DESSERT- Cook puddings.

FINAL PREPARATIONS
STARTER- Cook almonds, assemble oysters or salmon and bread.

MAIN- Reheat shanks, reheat mash, cook peas and beans, dress salad.

DESSERT- Warm puddings and sauce.

WINE- Serve a chilled sauvignon blanc with the starter, a gutsy shiraz or merlot blend with the shanks and a chilled bubbly with the dessert.

menu plan 4

LEEK, POTATO AND ROASTED GARLIC SOUP WITH BREADSTICKS

LAMB RACKS WITH BEETS AND ONIONS AND SWEET AND SOUR MUSTARD SEED SAUCE

THYME ROASTED POTATOES AND MINTED ZUCCHINI

INDIVIDUAL COCONUT PAVLOVAS

menu plan (5)

Cooking a meal for someone you don't know well is always daunting, especially if your guest happens to be an important client, your boss or a new in-law. In these situations we instinctively try too hard to please and make everything unduly difficult and complicated. Less is more. You need to aim for something really simple, smart and elegant that requires little last minute fuss.

Take a conservative stance – nothing too ethnic, spicy or unusual, and definitely no offal. Avoid dishes that need a lot of last minute attention – look to cook ahead and reheat, or go for a tender, lean, roasting cut that can be browned ahead and fired into the oven before serving. Your job at serving time should be assembly rather than actual cooking. Soup or salad are both good starter options.
For another dessert idea try the panna cotta with green fruit salad.

ADVANCE PREPARATIONS

WELL AHEAD
STARTER- Make breadsticks and store in an airtight container.
MAIN- Make sweet and sour mustard seed sauce (page 97) and chill (it keeps for weeks).
DESSERT- Make pavlovas up to 5 days ahead and store in an airtight container.

DAY BEFORE
STARTER- Make soup.

ON THE DAY
MAIN- Sear meat and chill, prepare onions, beets and potatoes for roasting, slice zucchini ready to cook.
DESSERT- Prepare mango passionfruit topping and chill, time vegetables to roast with meat.

FINAL PREPARATIONS
STARTER- Reheat soup and serve with breadsticks.

MAIN- Add meat to roasted vegetables, reheat sauce, cook zucchini.

DESSERT- Garnish pavlovas with mango passionfruit topping.

WINE- Serve a dry Spanish sherry with the soup, a cabernet blend with the lamb racks, and a chilled bubbly with the dessert.

149

BOWL OF SMOKY BABA GHANOUSH, MARINATED OLIVES AND PITA BREAD CRISPS

CRACKLING APPLE ROAST PORK WITH ALL THE TRIMMINGS

RUBY ROASTED PEARS

It's a great thing, tradition. Without it, what pattern would mark the important ceremonies and events in our lives and anchor our collective response? Tradition gives us surety, ever more important as the world races madly by. At the table we serve up tradition with a roast – carved at the table with all the trimmings.

If pork does not take your fancy, opt for a leg of lamb, a fillet of beef or a whole roast chicken.

Start off with something light – a platter of nibbles or a light, fresh salad. For dessert, fruit is the best option. When pears are out of season offer a green fruit salad or grilled fruits. Meringues are always welcome too.

ADVANCE PREPARATIONS

WELL AHEAD
STARTER- Marinate olives (they keep for months), make Pita Bread Crisps and store in an airtight container, make Smoky Baba Ghanoush up to 5 days ahead and chill.

DAY BEFORE
MAIN- Pork can be stuffed and covered with fennel rub a day ahead.
DESSERT- Poach pears ready to roast, make spiced mascarpone or Greek yogurt and chill.

ON THE DAY
MAIN- Prepare ingredients for pork and vegetables for roasting. Time pork cooking and any roast vegetables you plan to serve (pages 64 and 91).
DESSERT- Reduce syrup for pears.

FINAL PREPARATIONS
STARTER- Arrange starter platter.

MAIN- Finish cooking pork and vegetables and thicken sauce.

DESSERT- Turn up oven and roast pears.

WINE- Serve chilled bubbly with nibbles, pinot noir with pork and, if desired, a chilled sweet dessert wine with pears.

menu plan 6

A DINNER FOR ROMANCE p29 : p84 : p138

FRESHEST OYSTERS

SPICY CHICKEN TAGINE AND COUSCOUS (TO SHARE)

WHITE CHOCOLATE AND RASPBERRY PARFAIT

menu plan 7

It is important when planning a menu of seduction to consider the desired outcome. A menu to ignite the flame of passion needs to be light and tantalising.

If it's marriage you are after you'll need a different strategy. Aim straight for the heart with a spot of comfort food – steak and kidney pie or a good old-fashioned roast.

Even if you know someone well already, keep the play in the kitchen rather than in overwhelming formalities of lit candles and intimate table settings. It's much less stuffy to cook and talk and share spoons over the kitchen bench.

Oysters are an obvious starting point, even if you are chasing the marriage stakes. If you or your prospect don't like oysters either roasted scallops in the half shell or asparagus and scallop salad offer a luxurious yet light starter. Share a whole roasted poussin for a main course. Pasta with smoked salmon, capers and rocket (arugula), glazed chilli lime chicken, or the Mediterranean stuffed salmon fillets are all succulent, seductive main course dishes. For dessert it's hard to go past the silky pleasures of the parfait, but if your motives are towards the altar, the naughty tarte tatin is a real heart pleaser to woo the boys.

ADVANCE PREPARATIONS

WELL AHEAD
DESSERT- Make parfait and freeze. Make liqueur syrup, cover and chill.

DAY BEFORE
MAIN- For 2 people you'll need only 1 large or 2 small poussins, half the sauce and half the couscous. Marinate chicken overnight.

ON THE DAY
STARTER- Make dressing for the oysters.
MAIN- Time cooking of chicken, prepare couscous.

FINAL PREPARATIONS
STARTER- Serve oysters, allowing 4-6 each. Serve chilled in a bowl if shells aren't available.

MAIN- Cook beans, finish cooking chicken and heat couscous.

DESSERT- Assemble parfait.

WINE- Chilled bubbly throughout or a buttery chardonnay with the poussin.

CAESAR SALAD

FISH PIE

GARLICKY POTATO
GRATIN AND GREEN
BEANS

SYRUPY GRILLED FRUITS

If the housekeeping budget disappeared into those new Manolo Blahnik pumps this week, don't fret, you can still whip up a stylish, tasty feast.

Wine purchases aside, you'll likely spend the most money on animal protein. Reduce the amount of protein in a recipe and bulk up the plate or the dish with starchy vegetables such as pumpkin and potatoes. Shoestring gourmet tactics see ethnic flavours take reign – after all, some of the most delicious food in the world comes out of peasant kitchens.

Score the benefits of flavour and price by choosing peak season produce and opt for vegetarian dishes. This works really well with dishes such as curries and tagines. The laksa sauce, the Thai chicken curry sauce base or the sauce used in the spicy chicken tagine can each be prepared sans their relevant chicken, fish or meat, and chopped root vegetables, green beans or other seasonal vegetables used in their place.

Make a fish pie using fresh fish and a few hard-boiled eggs. If it's spring, fold some fresh asparagus into the sauce before baking. You could also serve mussels in any of the sauces given on page 35. In summer, pronto pasta with pine nuts and tomatoes is another good, cheap option.

ADVANCE PREPARATIONS

WELL AHEAD
STARTER- Prepare Caesar dressing and chill. Bake crostini and store in an airtight container.
DESSERT- Make syrup for fruit.

DAY BEFORE
STARTER- Wash and dry lettuce and store in a clean plastic bag in the fridge.
MAIN-Make fish pie ready to cook.

ON THE DAY
STARTER- Cook bacon for salad and shave parmesan into a bowl.
MAIN- Cook potato gratin ready to reheat, prepare green beans. Time cooking of pie.

FINAL PREPARATIONS
STARTER- Assemble and dress salad.

MAIN- Finish cooking pie, cook green beans, reheat gratin.

DESSERT- Grill fruit.

WINE- Ask people to bring a bottle. Riesling will be good with this menu.

menu plan 8

p36 : p20 : p42 : p18 : p132

SLOW ROASTED VINE
TOMATOES WITH FRESH
MOZZARELLA SALAD

TUSCAN ZUCCHINI SOUP
WITH FOCACCIA

BALSAMIC CARAMELISED
ONION TARTS WITH
ROCKET AND AVOCADO
SALAD

VANILLA PANNA COTTA
WITH GREEN FRUIT SALAD

menu plan 9

Vegetarian food has come a long way since the bland, heavy, cheesy lentil and beansprout offerings of the seventies. Here you will find a variety of satisfying and elegant options.

For many people, vegetarian food is a frequent approach to dining and diet rather than a stringent rule.

This four-course tasting menu offers some brilliant flavours. Use vegetable stock in place of chicken stock for the soup.

For a three-course menu, leave out the tomatoes and mozzarella.

ADVANCE PREPARATIONS

WELL AHEAD
FIRST COURSE- Make balsamic dressing.
SECOND COURSE- Make bread dough and chill or freeze.
THIRD COURSE- Make pastry and freeze, or buy commercial savoury pastry and freeze. Make caramelised onions and chill up to 2 weeks ahead.
DESSERT- Prepare dessert syrup and chill, make optional praline for dessert garnish and store in a closed container.

THE DAY BEFORE
SECOND COURSE- Make soup. Thaw bread dough in fridge.
DESSERT- Make panna cotta and chill.

ON THE DAY
FIRST COURSE- Slow roast tomatoes, marinate cheese.

SECOND COURSE- Bake bread.
THIRD COURSE- Cook onion tarts.
DESSERT- Make fruit salad and chill.

FINAL PREPARATIONS
FIRST COURSE- Plate up tomatoes and salad.

SECOND COURSE- Heat soup, add parmesan and parsley. Warm bread.

THIRD COURSE- Warm tarts, toss salad.

DESSERT- Garnish panna cotta with fruit and syrup.

WINES- Serve chilled sauvignon blanc with the tomatoes, a dry Spanish sherry or pinot gris with the soup, and a buttery chardonnay with the tart. For dessert you could have ice-cold bubbles or a chilled, sweet sticky wine.

KITCHEN ESSENTIALS

You don't need a lot of fancy equipment to produce great food. Unless you are really serious about cooking and wish to bone meat and fillet fish, a cook's knife will see you right for most jobs. Choose one made from good quality steel that feels comfortable and balanced in your hand. I find a 20cm knife suits my hand best. A bigger hand will find a bigger, heavier blade works better. Add a small, cheap paring knife and a serrated knife for bread. You may want to invest in a knife sharpener. A food processor is indispensable – you'll use it all the time. If you don't have one ask your mother, lover or Father Christmas for this useful gift.

A good heavy-based frypan and a large, heavy casserole-type dish that can be used on the stove-top and in the oven are both important. Remove thin-based pots and pans from your kitchen forever. Thin bases burn and buckle, making it impossible to cook anything evenly. Make sure your pots are big enough – to boil potatoes for eight people or cook a large pot of pasta.

Get a set of mixing bowls, storage containers for prepared ingredients, oven trays and a couple of decent-sized roasting dishes. Tool wise, you'll need a zester for citrus, a good grater, lemon juicer, kitchen scissors, can opener, fish slice, measuring spoons and cups, a heatproof jug, potato peeler, potato masher, slotted spoon and wooden spoon, whisk, pepper grinder and chopping board. Oh, and don't forget some tongs – you don't need asbestos fingers.

A mandolin or Benriner slicer makes fabulous matchstick, julienne and thin slices in a flash and is one of the few non-essentials that can really deliver that wow factor to food. But take care not to cut off your finger – the blades are incredibly sharp.

SHOPPING

This is probably the single most important part of the whole deal. Start with stale or limp ingredients and your job will always be hard. Support your local fresh food suppliers and tell them what you need. A good butcher will be happy to bone, stuff and trim or try to get special items in for you. The boys at The Meat Keeper where I get my meat are professional butchers. As such they not only know how to age meat properly but can tell me the best way to cook a certain cut or how long it might take in the oven.

It's the same with produce. You want really fresh produce, ideally organically grown, from suppliers whose systems you trust. Smell, touch and gently feel before you buy. Get to know when foods are in their natural season (some people may find it extraordinary that I am saying this but for many city dwellers who don't have gardens and know only the year-round supplies of supermarkets, the fact that corn ripens in summer and kiwifruit in winter may not be evident).

Eating with the seasons provides a pleasing rhythm that makes you feel connected and in touch with nature.

OVEN HEAT

From brand to brand and kitchen to kitchen, ovens cook differently. For this reason, and also because ingredients differ in their moisture content and ability to absorb liquid etc, you do need to use your judgement and treat the cooking times in recipes as a guide. I prefer to cook with a gas cooktop and electric fan-forced oven. Check 10-15% before the specified recipe cook time to see how things are proceeding. As you cook more you will see where your oven sits in relation to this book and will be able to judge how to amend cooking times accordingly. Remember, too, to preheat the oven to the temperature specified before you start cooking and that if you overload a domestic oven, the temperature will often drop and things will take longer to cook.

All the recipes in this book have been tested with a fan-forced oven. This heats up more quickly and tends to cook food more evenly than a conventional oven. Fan-forced ovens deliver about 15% more heat than conventional ovens so if you use a non-fan oven you may need to add about 10% to the cooking time or increase the heat by 5-10°C (10-20°F).

MEASURES USED IN THIS BOOK

1 cup equals 250ml (8.5 fl oz)
1 tbsp (tablespoon) equals 15ml
1 tsp (teaspoon) equals 5ml
A ruler can be found on the inside back flap.

SAVING ON WASHING UP

No one likes to be faced with a mountain of dishes. Wash up and tidy as you go while cooking – it's really hard to cook or think in a mess. Baking parchment is incredibly useful as a liner for roasting and baking to stop sticking and save on washing up. I use it wherever I can in oven cooking to line pans before pie making, grilling or roasting – unless I want the caramelisation created by juices in a roasting pan for some gravy.

Soak the mashed potato pot as soon as you've dished up. This stuff could stand in for glue.

Should you be unlucky enough to burn a pot, fill it with water, add 1 tsp dishwasher powder and boil for 5 minutes. Most burnt pots can be remedied in this way.

PANTRY

Having a well organised pantry is key to making good food without a lot of planning. Stocking your cupboard with ethnic ingredients allows you to be creative with very little forethought and ensures you will never be short of a flavour boost. For example, curry spices, poppadoms, lentils and rice have an Indian theme; extra virgin olive oil, balsamic and wine vinegars, anchovies, garlic, capers, tomato paste, polenta, oregano, canned tomatoes and pesto provide Mediterranean flavours; short grain rice, soy sauce, wasabi, dashi stock, miso, rice vinegar and seaweeds offer Japanese tangents; fish sauce, sesame oil, oyster sauce, ginger and kaffir lime leaves allow you to create Asian tones in your food. For browning, frying and general cooking use a commercial extra virgin olive oil and a flavourless oil such as grapeseed. Avocado oil is also a good all-purpose oil with a high burn temperature. Treat the very best estate virgin olive oil like gold and use it judiciously to add flavour and garnish where it will count. Sesame oil is very useful and walnut oil is divine but only when it's fresh – it goes rancid very quickly.

FREEZER

It's easy for a freezer to turn into a cemetery for dead food. That wild duck or side of salmon that someone gave you, the cheap deal on lamb fillets, the leftover oxtail casserole – it's all fabulous when it goes in there but if it lingers for more than 3 or 4 months (less for fish) it will quickly dry out and become horrid.

Useful items to keep in the freezer include ice, chicken stock, parmesan cheese, premium vanilla ice cream, pita bread and par-baked bread, spinach and peas, berries, smoked salmon, pesto and pastry.

Kaffir lime leaves and other tough-leafed herbs such as thyme freeze well. I also keep nuts in the freezer to stop them from going rancid (rancid foods contain carcinogens). Don't forget that you can freeze cooked beans or rice very successfully, so you may like to cook these in bulk for later use.

GLOSSARY

Coring tomatoes- use a sharp knife to cut the stem cores out of tomatoes; they are always tough and horrid.

Crispy fried shallots- available commercially from Asian food stores.

Dice- cut into 1cm / ½ inch cubes.

Fish Sauce- a strong smelling Asian condiment; use like soy sauce.

Fold- very gently combine mixtures with a large scooping motion, using a large, flat spoon.

Italian parsley- has a flat leaf. Regular parsley can be substituted.

Maryland- chicken leg quarter

Non-corrosive bowl- acid ingredients should never be put into aluminium or other corrosive metal bowls. Use a plastic or glass container.

Olive oil spray- buy commercially, or put olive oil into a spritzer.

Purée- blend until smooth.

Season- add salt and pepper to taste.

Sea salt- is usually coarser than fine salt and weighs less per spoonful.

Sesame oil- very useful to add flavour, especially in Asian cooking.

Sweet Thai chilli sauce- a very useful sweet commercial sauce.

Toasting nuts- either place on a baking tray and bake for 12-15 minutes at 180°C / 350°F, or microwave ½ cup at a time for 2-3 minutes, stirring every 30 seconds.

Zest- the thin, aromatic, oily outer skin of citrus fruits. Take care not to include the white pith underneath which is bitter.

INDEX